MODERN CIVIL AIRLINERS

Jonathan Falconer

JJN
PUBLISHING

First published in 2021

British Library Cataloguing in Publication Data
A catalogue record for this book is available from the British Library.

Printed book ISBN 978 1 8384277 0 2
ebook ISBN 978 1 8384277 1 9

Published by
JJN Publishing Ltd
www.jjnpublishing.com

Printed and bound in Malta

While every effort is taken to ensure the accuracy of the information given in this book, no liability can be accepted by the author or publisher for any errors in, or omissions from, the information given.

▼ Pilot's HUD on the Boeing 787 Dreamliner. Mach 0.86 at FL340 (34,000ft) westbound across the North Atlantic to New York on 30 January 2018. A Delta Air Lines Boeing 767 is visible at top right following the same track, with a vertical separation of 1,000ft. (Ian Black)

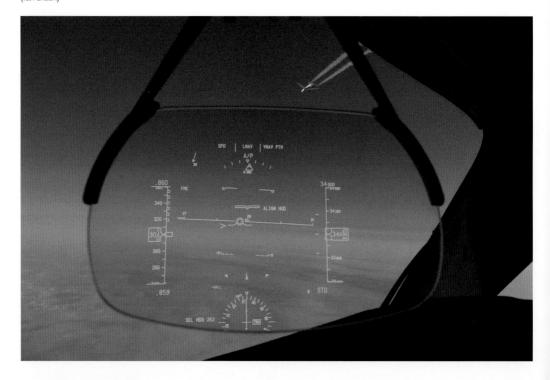

Contents

Introduction

The year 2020 brought the greatest challenge that the world airline and aerospace industry has faced in more than 100 years of its existence. An outbreak of a 'flu-like virus in a province in China in late 2019 quickly spread around the world and led to the World Health Organisation declaring a global pandemic the following March. The resulting Coronavirus lockdowns (or COVID-19, to use its correct term) and the mounting deaths from infection that followed forced long-haul air travel to almost grind to a halt, devastating revenues for airlines and plane builders alike. Within three months, passenger traffic across European airports had plummeted by 93% compared with June 2019.

Scheduled passenger flight activity for the Airbus A380 and Boeing 747 evaporated almost overnight, leading to the premature and sudden retirement of the 747 by the likes of British Airways, Virgin and Qantas. Many airlines announced swingeing cuts to their workforces and grounded whole classes of aircraft, particularly the fuel-hungry Boeing 747, Airbus A340 and A380 fleets, as well as deferring the purchase of new aircraft in a bid to conserve money.

Short-term savings were made by grounding fleets but, anticipating much smaller revenues over the next three years, airlines were forced to become leaner operations to survive. Many smaller carriers without the cash reserves of the bigger boys simply went out of business.

COVID-19 has also hit airlines that operate older, out-of-production types – the Boeing 737-300/400/500 family declined to around 160 examples by March 2020, with the 747, 757 and 767 down to roughly 20, 80 and 110 in-service passenger examples respectively, while some 80 MD-80s remained active.

In April 2020 Airbus announced it was slashing aircraft output from its factories by a third and planned instead to produce about 48 aircraft a month across its A320, A330 and A350 programmes. It had gone into the year with a goal of delivering about 880 aircraft, or an average of 73 per month. Boeing reported in July that it would stop making its classic 747 in 2022 and was considering making steep job cuts. The company had lost $2.4bn in the three months to 30 June 2020, as sales fell by 25% to $11.8bn.

This is the stark reality of the Coronavirus pandemic and how it has totally upended the aviation industry. There were signs of a limited bounce-back in services in spring 2021, but these were heavily restricted by governments tightening travel restrictions in response to emerging new COVID-19 variants. Some industry analysts have predicted it could take around three years to return to 2019 passenger levels. But the damage has already been done and the aviation world that emerges post-COVID will be a very different one.

◄ **Cathay Pacific Boeing 747-400, B-HUI, pictured at Hong Kong on 2 January 2012, looking south towards the cargo area and Lantau Island. The aircraft operated for 22 years with Cathay before it was taken out of service in 2016 and scrapped two years later.** (Ian Black)

It is against this troubling background that *Modern Civil Airliners* has been written and compiled. It covers all major airliners in revenue service on the eve of the pandemic in 2020, excluding business jets, air taxis and some lesser types such as the Antonov An-148

and Comac ARJ21 Xiangfeng regional jet airliners, and the Saab 2000 and Xian MA60 regional turboprops. The book is split into two sections – the first covers current airliners, the second legacy types that are recently out of service or in limited use.

A full technical specification is provided for each current airliner, while a more brief summary accompanies entries for the legacy types. This is followed by a concise résumé for all types, covering their design and service histories.

In a book of this size the room for descriptive text is necessarily limited, but it is hoped that, in conjunction with the exciting and varied photographs accompanying each entry, it will be possible to get a feel for the many and varied types of airliner in current service, and those legacy types that were once at the cutting edge of air travel.

◀ **British Airways Boeing 747-400 G-CIVJ was delivered to the airline in March 1997. It was withdrawn from use in March 2020 due to the COVID-19 pandemic and flown to Air Salvage International at Cotswold Airport (Kemble) on 14 April. G-CIVJ's last passenger service was a Miami–London-Heathrow repatriation flight for cruise ship passengers late on 5 April as BA9113.** (Graham Wasey)

▼ **Thwarted by COVID-19 – a row of grounded A350-900 jets belonging to Cathay Pacific at Hong Kong on 3 May 2020.** (Ian Black)

With the glittering runway lights of Osaka International (Itami) Airport stretching ahead, a Boeing 737-800 begins its take-off run on 2 January 2017. The airport's scheduled passenger air traffic is in fact entirely domestic despite its 'international' designation. (motive56/Shutterstock)

PART ONE

CURRENT AIRLINERS

ATR 42/72

Lush tropical vegetation forms the backdrop as ATR 72-500, 9M-FYG, of Firefly climbs out of Langkawi International Airport that serves the Malaysian island of Langkawi in the Malacca Strait, 29 March 2019. Firefly provides connections to various points within Malaysia, southern Thailand, Singapore and Sumatra, Indonesia. (Phuong D. Nguyen/Shutterstock)

ATR 42/72

Country of origin: France/Italy.

Type: regional narrow-body twin-turboprop airliner.

Variants: ATR 42-300/400/500/600, ATR 42-600S (STOL); ATR 72-500/600, ATR 72-600F (Freighter).

First flight: ATR 42 – 16 August 1984; ATR 72 – 27 October 1988.

Produced: ATR 42 – 1984 to present; ATR 72 – 1988 to present.

Number delivered: ATR 42 – 486 (2020); ATR 72 – 1,234 (2020).

First introduced: ATR 42 – 3 December 1985 with Air Littoral; ATR 72 – 27 October 1989 with Finnair.

Main users: ATR 42 – Canadian North, EasyFly, FedEx Feeder, First Air, Silver Airways, Swiftair; ATR 72 – FedEx Feeder, Nordic Regional Airlines, Silver Airways, Wings Air, Azul Linhas Aéreas Brasileiras, Air New Zealand, IndiGo, Swiftair.

Powerplant: ATR 42-300 – 2 × 1,800hp/1,900hp Pratt & Whitney PW120/121; ATR 42-400 – 2 × 1,980hp PW121A; ATR 42-500/600 – 2 × 2,160hp PW127E/M; ATR 72 – 2 × 2,475hp Pratt & Whitney PW127F/M turboprops.

Performance: cruising speed, ATR 42-300 – 311mph (M0.41, 500kmh), ATR 42-400 – 300mph (M0.39, 484kmh), ATR 42-500/600 – 345mph (M0.45, 556kmh), ATR72 – 317mph (M0.41, 510kmh); ceiling, ATR42/ATR72, 25,000ft (7,620m); range, ATR 42-300 – 459nm (850km), ATR 42-400 – 794nm (1,470km), ATR 42-500/600 – 716nm (1,326km): ATR 72 – 785nm (1,454km), ATR 72-600F – 900nm (1,667km).

Weights: max take-off weight, ATR 42 – 18,600kg (41,005lb), ATR 72 – 22,000kg (48,501lb); max landing weight, ATR 42 – 18,300kg (40,344lb), ATR 72 – 21,850kg (48,170lb); max fuel capacity, ATR 42 – 1,500 US gals (5,680 litres), ATR 72 – 11,023lb (5,000 litres).

Dimensions: span, ATR 42 – 80ft 7in (24.57m), ATR 72 – 88ft 9in (27.05m); length overall, ATR 42 – 74ft 5in (22.67m), ATR 72 – 89ft 2in (27.17m); height, ATR 42 – 24ft 11in (7.59m), ATR 72 – 25ft 1in (7.65m).

Accommodation: flight crew of 2, single-aisle single-class seating, ATR 42 – 30 to 50, ATR 72 – 44 to 78.

Losses: ATR 42 – 34 hull losses and 276 fatalities; ATR 72 – 29 hull losses and 398 fatalities.

▼ A unique feature common to both the ATR 42 and ATR 72 is the propeller brake on No 2 engine, which means the engine can be used as an Auxiliary Power Unit (APU) on the ground at airfields without ground power. This is Czech Airlines ATR 42-500 at Prague Airport on 1 April 2012. (Petr Bonek/Shutterstock)

Notes: Developed as a result of a joint venture signed in 1981 between Aérospatiale of France (now known as Airbus) and Aeritalia of Italy (now called Leonardo) for a successor to the ageing Fokker F-27 Friendship and Handley Page Herald in the regional sector, the initial design focused on the 40-seat market and the result was the ATR 42. The initial flight of the prototype was on 16 August 1984 and the first commercial flight was with launch customer Air Littoral in December that year.

The name of the new aircraft in Italian was Aerei da Trasporto Regionale, or Avions de transport régional in French – with the acronym 'ATR' conveniently fitting both languages.

Developed in parallel with the ATR 42, the stretched version was named the ATR 72 and designed to carry 78 passengers. It boasted a 15ft increase in fuselage length and a wider wingspan to allow for 10% greater fuel capacity. The first flight was on 27 October 1988 with launch customer Air Littoral making its inaugural commercial service with the ATR 72 on 27 October 1989. Improvements and upgrades to the original ATR 42 specification were made with the -300 and -320 variants, which introduced more powerful PW121 engines. A further development was the ATR 42-300QC (Quick Change) or combi, whereby it can be quickly switched from

▲ The ATR 42-300QC (Quick Change or Combi) can be swiftly changed from passenger to cargo configuration thanks to the modular seating installation. Note the open forward cargo door. This is Hello Airlines' -300QC, S2-AHI, at Dhaka, Bangladesh, on 21 March 2017. (Shadman Samee/Creative Commons)

passenger to cargo carrying thanks to the modular seating installation. The next major change to the basic ATR 42 design was the -500 variant in 1995 that offered performance improvements, six-bladed propellers and increased passenger comfort. Dedicated cargo conversion programmes have also seen first-generation ATR 42 and ATR 72 aircraft being given a new lease of life, stripping out passenger interiors and converting them to freighters. The ATR 42/72 family has been sold around the world and goes from strength to strength, with its largest take-up from airlines in the Asia-Pacific region and Europe. The -600 series is the current production version for both types, featuring PW127M engines, performance improvements, an all-glass cockpit with wide screens and improved passenger cabin interior. In 2019 ATR announced the launch of its ATR 42-600S short take-off and landing variant, and the following year the ATR 72-600 freighter was introduced into commercial service with a capacity of 75.5cu m for both bulk cargo and unit load device configurations.

AIRBUS A220

A pair of Swiss Airbus A220-300s pass each other on the taxiway at Zurich Airport on 22 July 2020. The -300 complements the Airbus A319neo in competing with the Boeing 737 MAX-7. (Markus Mainka/Shutterstock)

Airbus A220

Country of origin: Canada.
Type: narrow-body twin-engine medium-range jet airliner.
Variants: A220-100/300.
First flight: 16 September 2013.
Produced: 2012 to present.
Number delivered: 155 (at April 2021).
First introduced: 15 July 2016 with Swiss International Air Lines.
Main users: Air Canada, airBaltic, EgyptAir, Air Senegal, Air Austral, Delta Air Lines, Swiss International Air Lines, jetBlue.
Powerplant: 2 × 19,000–23,300lbf Pratt & Whitney PW1500G high-bypass geared turbofan engines.
Performance: max speed, 541mph (M0.71, 871kmh); cruising speed, 515mph (M0.67, 829kmh); ceiling 41,000ft (12,500m); range, A220-100 – 3,400nm (6,297km), A220-300 – 3,350nm (6,204km).
Weights: max ramp weight, A200-100 – 63,500kg (139,993lb), A200-300 – 70,300kg (154,985lb); max take-off weight, A220-100 – 63,100kg (139,000lb), A200-300 – 69,900kg (154,103lb); max landing weight, A200-100 – 52,400kg (115,522lb), A200-300 – 58,700kg (129,411lb); max zero fuel weight, A200-100 – 50,400kg (111,113lb), A200-300 – 55,800kg (123,018lb); max fuel capacity, A200-100 – 5,760 US gals (21,805 litres), A200-300 – 5,681 US gals (21,508 litres).
Dimensions: span, 115ft 1in (35.10m); length overall, A220-100 – 114ft 9in (35.00m), A220-300 – 127ft 0in (38.70m); fuselage diameter, 12ft 2in (3.70m); height, 38ft 8in (11.50m).
Accommodation: flight crew of 2, single-aisle 2-class seating 120 max (A220-100), 150 max (A220-300).
Losses: hull losses – 0, fatalities – 0.

▼ **An airBaltic Airbus A220-300 (Bombardier CS300) in custom livery takes off from Riga International Airport on a freezing January day in 2019.** (Karlis Dambrans/Shutterstock)

Notes: Originally known as the Bombardier C Series, the narrow-body jet airliner programme was launched in 2004 by Canada's Bombardier Aerospace to rival the McDonnell Douglas MD-80 series, Fokker 100, Boeing 737 Classic and BAe 146 in the 100–150-seat market. It was developed into the 110–120-seat CS100 and the 120–150-seat CS300 and became one of the first airliner types to adopt the new Pratt & Whitney geared turbofan engine, offering significant fuel savings and reduced ground noise. Its use of lightweight composite materials and enhanced aerodynamics also contributed to the type's lower operating costs. Single-aisle cabin seating is usually configured 2-3 in economy class and 2-2 in business class.

The CS100 made its maiden flight from Mirabel Airport on 16 September 2013, followed on 27 February 2015 by the CS300 prototype. On 29 June 2016 the first C Series, the CS100, was delivered to Swiss Global Air Lines, followed on 28 November by the first CS300 to airBaltic. Development costs for the C Series had spiralled out of control and led in 2018 to Bombardier selling the C Series programme to its competitor Airbus. On 20 July 2018, the CS100 was renamed the Airbus A220-100 and the CS300 the Airbus A220-300. The programme is now owned by a partnership between Airbus and the Quebec Government – Airbus Canada Limited Partnership.

By the end of 2019 some 100 A220s were in service around the world with airlines that included airBaltic, Air Canada, Air Tanzania, Delta Air Lines, Egyptair, Korean Air and Swiss International Air Lines.

During the global Coronavirus pandemic in 2020 the A220 came into its own, benefiting from its small size and low overheads, coupled with operating capabilities that rivalled larger airliners such as the Airbus A320 and Boeing 737. These characteristics proved attractive to airlines looking to slash costs while maintaining a minimal flight schedule flying fewer passengers more economically through the COVID-19 crisis. Take for example the US carrier Delta Air Lines, which parked all 62 of its 157-seat A320s but still flew its 31 109-seat A220-100s. An added bonus is that the small A220-100s can fly nearly 100 miles further than the A320s.

Airbus demonstrators display the company's complete single-aisle A320 family. All have essentially the same airframe apart from fuselage length and detail of the landing gear. (Airbus)

Airbus A320 family

The A320 is a single family of aircraft that comes in four sizes – A318, A319, A320 and A321. It was the first civil aircraft to pioneer fly-by-wire technology and is the only single-aisle aircraft capable of loading pallets and containers on its lower deck. The A320 family is the widest single-aisle fuselage aircraft on the market and all members have the same optimised cabin cross-section.

Airbus A318

Country of origin: EU.
Type: narrow-body jet airliner.
Variants: A318 only.
First flight: 15 January 2002.
Produced: 2003–13.
Number delivered: 80 (at JApril 2021).
First introduced: 22 July 2003 with Frontier Airlines.
Main users: Air France, TAROM, British Airways.
Powerplant: 2 × 23,800lbf Pratt & Whitney PW6122A/6124A or 2 × 23,300lbf CFM International CFM56-5B8/9 high-bypass turbofan engines.
Performance: max speed, 541mph (M0.71, 871kmh); max altitude, 39,100–41,000ft (11,900–12,500m); range, 3,100nm (5,750km).
Weights: max ramp weight, 68,400kg; max take-off weight, 68,000kg; max landing weight, 57,500kg; max zero fuel weight, 54,500kg; max fuel capacity, 6,400 US gals (24,210 litres).
Dimensions: span, 111ft 11in (34.10m); length overall, 103ft 2in (31.44m); fuselage width, 13ft 0in (3.95m); height, 41ft 2in (12.56m).
Accommodation: flight crew of 2, single-aisle max seating 132, typical 2-class seating 90–110.
Losses: hull losses – 0, fatalities – 0.

▼ British Airways launched its daily Club World service with the A318 from London-City Airport to New York-JFK in September 2009 and soon increased it to twice daily, although this was pared back to one flight per day in 2016. The service ceased in 2020. This is BA's A318, G-EUNB, on the stand at JFK on 9 July 2010. (Roland Arhelger/ Creative Commons)

Notes: Following its first flight on 15 January 2002, the A318 entered revenue service in July 2003 with US low-cost carrier Frontier Airlines. Carrying between 107 and 132 passengers, the A318 has a range of 3,100nm (5,700km) and although it is the smallest member of the Airbus family and has the shortest fuselage, it still offers a high level of passenger comfort with the widest single-aisle cabin available.

It is used primarily on short, low-density sectors between medium-sized cities, but its lighter weight and greater operating range means it can serve some routes that its sister the A320 would be unable to service such as London to New York, Perth to Auckland and Singapore to Tokyo.

Like other members of the A320 family it benefits from cockpit commonality, helping to reduce the cost of training, maintenance and operation of the aircraft. Pilots are qualified to fly any member of the A320 family with the common type rating.

During its development phase the A318 was affected after 9/11 by a fall in demand for new aircraft coupled with problems concerning the new Pratt & Whitney turbofan engine burning more fuel than was expected. Many customers who had opted

▲ TAROM's Airbus A318-111, YR-ASC, touches down on the wet runway at Istanbul-Ataturk Airport on 4 March 2018. (Evren Kalinbacak/Shutterstock)

for the A318 chose the A319 or A320 instead. Sales of the A318 were slow and by the time the last aircraft was completed in 2013 just 80 had been delivered, making it only marginally better than its direct competitor the Boeing 737-600. In 2007 the A318 was certified by the European Aviation Safety Agency (EASA) to land at steeper-than-usual gradients, approving a 5.5-degree approach slope compared to a nominal 3-degree slope for standard operations. This potential to transform long-haul services between city centres was shown when British Airways operated two A318s on an exclusive transatlantic business class service between London City Airport and New York-JFK via Shannon to refuel and clear US customs and immigration. The route was launched in 2009, suspended in March 2020 and finally withdrawn from BA's timetables in August. As of June 2020, 37 of the 80 A318s built remain in service, Air France being the largest operator with 18 aircraft. Of the remaining 43, 23 have been scrapped and 20 are stored.

Airbus A319ceo/A319neo

Country of origin: EU.

Type: narrow-body jet airliner.

Variants: A319ceo/A319neo/A319CJ/A319LR.

First flight: 25 August 1995.

Produced: 1994 to present.

Number delivered: A319ceo – 1,482 (at January 2021); A319neo – 3 (at January 2021).

First introduced: April 1996 with Swissair.

Main operators: A319ceo – American Airlines, Delta Air Lines, easyJet, United Airlines; A319neo – Spirit Airlines, Air China.

Powerplant: A319ceo – 2 × 22,000–27,000lbf CFM International CFM56-5 or 2 × IAE V2500A5; A319neo – 2 × 24,100lbf Pratt & Whitney PurePower PW1100G-JM turbofan or 2 × CFM International LEAP-1A high-bypass turbofan engines.

Performance: max speed, 541mph (M0.71, 871kmh); cruising speed, 515mph (M0.67, 829kmh); max altitude, A319ceo – 39,100–41,000ft (11,900–12,500m), A319neo – 39,100–39,800ft (11,900–12,100m); range, A319ceo – 3,750nm (6,950km), A319neo – 3,700nm (6,850km), A319LR – 4,500nm (8,300km).

Weights: max ramp weight, 75,900kg (167,330lb); max take-off weight, 75,500kg (166,000lb); max landing weight, A319ceo – 62,500kg (138,000lb), A319neo – 63,900kg (140,875lb); max zero fuel weight, A319ceo – 60,300kg (132,938lb), A319neo – 58,500kg (129,000lb); max fuel capacity, A319ceo – 7,980 US gals (30,190 litres), A319neo – 7,060 US gals (26,730 litres).

Dimensions: span, 117ft 5in (35.80m); length overall, 111ft 0in (33.84m); fuselage width, 13ft 0in (3.95m); height, 38ft 7in (11.76m).

Accommodation: flight crew of 2, max seating, A319ceo – 156, typical 2-class seating 110–140, A319neo – max seating 160, typical 2-class seating 120–150.

Losses: A319ceo – hull losses – 3, fatalities – 0. A319neo – hull losses – 0, fatalities – 0.

▼ easyJet's Airbus A319ceo, G-EZAX, taxies at London-Luton Airport on 9 July 2019. After nearly 14 years with easyJet, this aircraft passed to United Airlines on 1 May 2020 as N832OU. (Markus Mainka/Shutterstock)

Notes: The A319 is the shortened-fuselage version of the A320 and first entered revenue service in April 1996 with Swissair. With a fuselage seven frames shorter, the overall length is reduced by 5ft 3in (1.60m) ahead of the wing, and 7ft 0in (2.13m) behind. Seating capacity is thus reduced accordingly, typically to 124–145. It shares a common type rating with all other members of the A320 family. Other changes include elimination of the bulk cargo-hold door and the forward over-wing emergency exit. The A319ceo featured de-rated engines that were almost identical to the more powerful versions fitted to the A320.

Not only is the A319 popular with low-cost airlines, it is also a favourite among governments and business customers who operate 74 of the type. A small number of specialised variants have also been built – the A319CJ corporate jet, with increased range and ceiling, and the option to configure the cabin for up to 39 passengers or as few as eight. Custom fittings can include a fully equipped office, dining room, bedroom, bathroom and a shower. The A319LR version offers an increased range of up to 4,500nm (8,300km) compared to 3,750nm (6,950km) for the basic A319ceo.

▲ The LR version of the A319 offers an extra 750 miles of range compared with the A319ceo. Here is Qatar Airways' Airbus A319-133LR, A7-CJA, on short finals to Chiang Mai International Airport, Thailand, on 8 November 2015. (Sudpoth Sirirattanasakul/Shutterstock)

In January 1997 an A319 broke a record during a delivery flight by flying 3,588nm (6,645km) in 9 hours 5 minutes on the great circle route to Winnipeg, Manitoba, from Hamburg, Germany. The new engine option (neo) variant of the A319 made its first flight on 31 March 2017, offering seating for 110 to 140 passengers in two classes, or up to 156 in a high-density configuration, with a range of up to 3,700nm. Aerodynamic improvements to the A319neo include large curved winglets (Sharklets), weight savings and two choices of new-generation turbofan engines, which combined give 15% lower fuel consumption and 8% lower operating costs, as well as environmental benefits of reduced noise and emissions when compared to the A320 series. In July 2020, some 1,406 A319s were in service with 108 airlines; American Airlines, easyJet and United Airlines operated the largest fleets with 133, 123 and 86 aircraft respectively.

Airbus A320ceo/A320neo

Country of origin: EU.
Type: narrow-body jet airliner.
Variants: A320ceo/A320neo.
First flight: 22 February 1987.
Produced: 1986 to present.
Number delivered: A320ceo – 4,752 (at January 2021), A320neo – 1,157 (at January 2021).
First introduced: A320ceo – 1988 with Air France, A320neo – May 2017 with Virgin America.
Main operators: A320ceo – Aeroflot, Air Asia, Alaska Airlines, Allegiant Air, British Airways, China Eastern Airlines, China Southern Airlines, Delta Air Lines, easyJet, IndiGo, jetBlue, Jetstar Airways, LATAM Airlines, Lufthansa, Shenzhen Airlines, Sichuan Airlines, Spirit Airlines, Spring Airlines, United Airlines, Vueling Airlines, Wizz Air Hungary; A320neo – Air Asia, Air India, Azul Brazilian Airlines, China Eastern Airlines, China Southern Airlines, easyJet, Frontier Airlines, GoAir, IndiGo, Lufthansa, Pegasus Airlines, SAS, Vueling Airlines.
Powerplant: A320ceo – 2 × 22,000lbf–27,000lbf CFM International CFM56-5A or 2 × IAE V2500A5-high-bypass turbofan engines; A320neo – 2 × 27,120lbf Pratt & Whitney PurePower PW1100G-JM or 2 × CFM LEAP-1A.
Performance: max speed, 541mph (M0.71, 871kmh); cruising speed, 515mph (M0.67, 829kmh);

range 3,350nm (6,200km) with Sharklets; ceiling, A320ceo – 39,100–41,000ft (11,900m–12,500m), A320neo – 39,100–39,800ft (11,900–12,100m); range, 3,400nm (6,300km).
Weights: max ramp weight, A320ceo – 78,400kg (172,840lb), A320neo – 79,400kg (175,050lb); max take-off weight, A320ceo – 78,000kg (172,000lb), A320neo – 79,000kg (174,200lb); max landing weight, A320ceo – 66,000kg (145,505lb), A320neo – 67,400kg (148,590lb); max zero fuel weight, A320ceo – 62,500kg (137,790lb), A320neo – 64,300kg (141,760lb); max fuel capacity, A320ceo – 7,190 US gals (27,200 litres), A320neo – 7,060 US gals (26,730 litres).
Dimensions: span, 117ft 5in (35.80m) with Sharklets; length overall, 123ft 3in (37.57m); fuselage width, 13ft 0in (3.95m); height, 38ft 7in (11.76m).
Accommodation: flight crew of 2, single-aisle, A320ceo – max seating 180, typical 2-class seating 140–170, A320neo – max seating 194, typical 2-class seating 150–180.
Losses: A320ceo – hull losses – 37, fatalities – 1,113. A320neo – hull losses – 0, fatalities – 0.

▼ A comparison of rivals – Virgin America's Airbus A320ceo, N623VA, and in the foreground United's Boeing 737-900ER (N37427). (Bill Larkins/Creative Commons)

Notes: At the time of its programme launch in 1984, the first single-aisle Airbus, the A320, was the only completely new 'clean sheet of paper' jet airliner design anywhere in the Western world. Conceived as a family of aircraft offering a full spectrum of range and capacity, it was also the world's first airliner designed with a digital fly-by-wire flight control system, with pilot inputs through a novel side-stick control rather than the traditional control yoke. It was followed by the longer Airbus A321 in 1993, the shorter A319 (1995) and the shorter-still A318 in 2002. Fuel efficiency with the chosen CFM56-5 and IAE V2500 turbofans was achieved by using composite materials in the aircraft's primary structures, centre-of-gravity control was achieved using fuel transfer and the glass cockpit and two-pilot crew operation made the A320 an attractive proposition to airlines around the world. More than 9,400 of the A320 family of aircraft have been ordered and some 5,400 delivered to more than 380 customers and operators worldwide, making it the most successful single-aisle jet airliner.

The A320 cabin can be configured for several seating options, but it usually seats between 140 and 170 passengers, with a maximum capacity of 180. The single-aisle cabin is also wider than its original

▲ British Airways' Airbus CFM LEAP-1A-powered A320neo (G-TTNA) at London-Heathrow Airport on 1 August 2018. (Lukas Wunderlich/Shutterstock)

competitors the Boeing 737 and 757, with an external fuselage diameter of 13ft 0in (3.95m) compared to 12ft 3in (3.80m) of the two Boeings. A ground-breaking new feature of the A320 was the cabin inter-communication data system (CIDS), wiring up PA speakers, lighting, reading lamps, entertainment system, crew intercom and cabin safety signs. CIDS did away with the need for extensive and costly re-cabling required for changes in cabin sizes and classes, instead using a software solution that took just minutes to effect. The A320neo (new engine option) launched in 2017 features the latest Pratt & Whitney PurePower PW1100 and CFM LEAP-1A turbofans, large wingtip aerodynamic devices (Sharklets) and new 'Airspace' cabin design. The A320neo family delivers a 20% fuel saving per seat over the A320ceo together with up to 500nm (900km) of extra range, or 2 tonnes of extra payload.

Since its launch in 2010, the A320 family has received more than 8,677 orders from more than 100 customers, making it the world's best-selling single-aisle aircraft.

Airbus A321ceo/A321neo

Country of origin: EU.

Type: narrow-body jet airliner.

Variants: A321-100ceo/200ceo/A321neo/neoLR.

Number delivered: A321ceo – 1,766 (at January 2021), A321neo – 469 (at January 2021).

First flight: A321ceo – 11 March 1993, A321neo – 9 February 2016.

Produced: 1986 to present.

Entered service: A321ceo – January 1994 with Lufthansa, A321neo – 31 May 2017 with Virgin America.

Main operators: Air China, Air New Zealand, Alaska Airlines, All Nippon Airways, American Airlines, British Airways, China Southern Airlines, China Eastern Airlines, Delta Air Lines, easyJet, Frontier Airlines, jetBlue, Lufthansa, Turkish Airlines, Vietnam Airlines.

Powerplant: A3231ceo – 2 × 30,000–33,000lbf CFM International CFM56-5B or 2 × IAE V2500A5; A321neo – 2 × 33,110lbf Pratt & Whitney PurePower PW1100G-JM and CFM LEAP-1A; A321LR – 2 × 33,000lbf PW1133G-JM high-bypass turbofan engines.

Performance: max speed, 541mph (M0.71, 871kmh); cruising speed, 515mph (M0.67, 829kmh); max altitude, 39,100–39,800ft (11,900–12,100m); range, A321ceo – 3,212nm (5,950km), A321neo – 4,000nm (7,400km).

Weights: max ramp weight, A321ceo – 93,900kg (207,014lb), A321neo – 97,400kg (214,730lb); max take-off weight, A321ceo – 93,500kg (206,132lb), A321neo – 97,000kg (213,800lb); max landing weight, A321ceo – 77,800kg (171,519lb), A321neo – 79,200kg (174,606lb); max zero fuel weight, A321ceo – 73,800kg (162,701lb), A321neo – 75,600kg (166,670lb); max fuel capacity, A321ceo – 7,935 US gals (30,030 litres), A321neo – 8,700 US gals (32,940 litres).

Dimensions: span, 117ft 5in (35.80m) with Sharklets; length overall, 146ft 0in (44.51m); fuselage width, 13ft 0in (3.95m); height, 38ft 7in (11.76m).

Accommodation: flight crew of 2, max seating, A321ceo – 220, typical 2-class seating 170–210, A321neo – 244, typical 2-class seating 180–220, A321LR – single-class up to 206.

Losses: A321ceo – hull losses – 9, fatalities – 377; A321neo – hull losses – 0, fatalities – 0.

▼ In mid-2020, China Eastern Airlines operated a fleet of 77 Airbus A321ceo aircraft. Here A321-200, B-8648, lands at Shanghai Hongqiao Airport on 28 September 2019, while in the background another A321-200 (B-6330) taxies. At the right is a Juneyao Air Boeing 787-9 Dreamliner. (Markus Mainka/ Shutterstock)

Notes: On 22 May 1989 Airbus announced that it was going to offer a stretched A320 known as the A321, with passenger capacity increased to 220. The programme was launched on 24 November 1989 and flight-testing began on 11 March 1993. Two high-bypass turbofan engine choices were included – IAE V2500-A5 rated at 29,000lbf and CFM56-5B1 at 30,000lbf. The first A321ceo entered service in January 1994 with Lufthansa.

The most obvious change compared to the A320 is the lengthened fuselage, achieved with a 14ft 0in (4.27m) plug ahead of the wing and an 8ft 9in (2.67m) plug aft. Each fuselage plug includes a left/ right pair of emergency exits. The wing is reinforced, the trailing edge is extended in chord with addition of double-slotted flaps and the main landing gears are strengthened to cope with the increased maximum landing weight of 77,800kg (171,519lb).

Airbus announced a new engine option (neo) version of the A321 in December 2010, which featured (in addition to the new Pratt & Whitney PurePower PW1100G-JM and CFM LEAP-1A engines) airframe improvements and winglets (or Sharklets in Airbus's parlance), and capacity for 24 more passengers. Airbus's new Cabin-Flex option increased the A321neo's maximum certified capacity to 244 seats, while maintaining a minimum

▲ **Arkia Israeli Airlines was the launch customer in November 2018 for the Airbus A321LRneo. This is 4X-AGK at Ben Gurion Airport on 21 December the same year.** (Micha/ Creative Commons)

comfort standard of at least 18in-wide seats. On 31 May 2017 the A321neo was delivered to its first customer, Virgin America.

The A321LR variant launched on 13 January 2015 provides extended range for the A320 family's longest-fuselage version, capable of flying routes of up to 4,000nm with 206 passengers by utilising extra fuel carried in three additional centre tanks (ACTs). In October 2018, the A321LR's long-range capability was formally certified by the European Aviation Safety Agency (EASA) and US Federal Aviation Administration (FAA). Ideally suited to transatlantic routes, the A321LR allows airlines to exploit new long-haul markets that were previously not accessible with current single-aisle aircraft. Operators can outfit its cabin in state-of-the-art 2-class configurations, including full-flat seats for true long-haul comfort, or in a single-class layout.

Launch customer Arkia Israeli Airlines took delivery of the first A321LR in November 2018. An A321XLR is planned for 2023 with even greater range (up to 4,700nm, 8,700km) in a 2-class layout.

AIRBUS A330CEO/A330NEO

Brand-new Airbus A330-900neo, PR-ANZ, operated by Azul Linhas Aéreas Brasileiras following its inaugural flight in Recife-Guararapes International Airport, Brazil, on 1 June 2019.

(Thiago B. Trevisan/Shutterstock)

Airbus A330ceo/A330neo

Country of origin: EU.

Type: wide-body jet airliner.

Variants: A330-200/200F/300/300P2F/800neo/900neo.

Number delivered: 1,512 (at January 2021).

First flight: A330-200 – 2 November 1992; A330-800neo/900neo – 19 October 2017.

Entered service: 17 January 1994 with Air Inter.

Main operators: Aer Lingus, Aeroflot, Air Canada, Air China, Air France, Air Portugal, Asiana, Cathay Dragon, Cathay Pacific, China Airlines, China Eastern Airlines, China Southern Airlines, Delta Air Lines, EVA Airways, Garuda Indonesia, Hainan Airlines, Korean Air, Malaysia Airlines, Qatar Airways, Saudi Arabian Airlines, Sichuan Airlines, Sri Lankan Airlines, Turkish Airlines.

Powerplant: A330-200/300 – 2 × 64,500–71,000lbf GE CF6 (except 200F)/PW4000/Rolls-Royce Trent 700 high-bypass turbofans; A330-800neo/900neo – 2 × 72,834lbf Rolls-Royce Trent 7000-72.

Performance: max speed, A330-200/300/800neo/900neo – 570mph (M0.74, 918kmh); cruising speed, A330-200/300 – 541mph (M0.71, 871kmh); service ceiling, A330-200/300 – 40,000ft (12,500m), A330-800neo/900neo – 41,450ft (12,634m); range, A330-200 – 7,250nm (13,450km), A330-300 – 6,350nm (11,750km), A330-800neo – 8,150nm (15,094km), A330-900neo – 7,200nm (13,334km).

Weights: max ramp weight, A330-200/300 – 242,900kg (535,500lb), A330-800neo/900neo – 251,900kg (555,344lb); max take-off weight, A330-200/300 – 242,000kg (533,520lb), A330-800neo/900neo – 251,000kg (553,360lb); max landing weight, A330-200 – 182,000kg (401,240lb), A330-300 – 187,000kg (412,260lb), A330-800neo – 186,000kg (410,060lb), A330-900neo – 191,000kg (421,080lb); max zero fuel weight, A330-200 – 170,000kg (374,785lb), A330-300 – 175,000kg (385,810lb), A330-800neo – 176,000kg (388,010lb), A330-900neo – 181,000kg (399,040lb); max fuel capacity, A330-200/300/900neo – 36,750 US gals (139,090 litres), A330-800neo – 36,750 US gals (139,000 litres).

Dimensions: span, A330-200/300 – 197ft 10in (60.30m), A330-800neo/900neo – 210ft 0in (64m); length overall, A330-300/900neo – 208ft 10in (63.66m), A330-200/800 – 193ft 0in (58.82m); fuselage width, A330-200/300/800neo/900neo –

▼ **Rolls-Royce Trent-powered Airbus A330-200 (VP-BLX) operated by Russian state airline Aeroflot, pictured at Miami on 6 July 2020.** (Ian Black)

18ft 6in (5.64m), height, A330-300/900neo – 55ft 1in (16.79m); A330-200/800neo – 57ft 1in (17.39m).
Accommodation: flight crew of 2, max seating, A330-300 – 440, typical 3-class 250–290, A330-200/800neo – 406, typical 210–250, 220–260, A330-900neo – 440, typical 3-class 260–300.
Losses: hull losses – 13, fatalities – 339.

▲ Airbus A330-300, G-VGEM, is one of six -300s operated by Virgin Atlantic. V-GEM is leased from AerCap, the largest owner of commercial aircraft in the world. 'Diamond Girl' is seen at London-Heathrow Airport on 31 July 2018. The -300s were used on Virgin's London-Heathrow to Hong Kong, Tokyo-Narita and Johannesburg services. (Markus Mainka/Shutterstock)

Notes: The wide-body twin-aisle twinjet Airbus A330 was developed in parallel with the company's A340 quadjet and was launched in June 1987. It was the first airliner from Airbus to offer a choice of three powerplants – GE CF6, PW4000 and the Rolls-Royce Trent 700. Typically carrying 277 passengers in a 3-class configuration, the first version, the A330-300, made its initial flight on 2 November 1992, with the first production model entering service with Air Inter on 17 January 1994. Four years later on 29 May 1998, the short-fuselage extended-range A330-200 made its inaugural flight with Canada 3000.

A dedicated mid-size cargo version of the A330-200, the 200F, was launched in 2007 and can carry 65,000kg of freight over 4,000nm (7,400km). It has a fuselage derived from the A300-600F, with no passenger windows and the same upward-hinged portside cargo door. Also, a small number of A330-300P2F freighter conversions were built. These are particularly suited to express delivery and e-commerce, and capable of transporting up to 62,000kg (137,000lb) of cargo.

On 1 June 2011 the first A330 Multi Role Tanker Transports (MRTT) was delivered to the Royal Australian Air Force. By 2020, 42 examples had been delivered to a number of other world air forces.

The new-generation A330-900neo flew for the first time on 19 October 2017, with its smaller sibling the 800neo following one year later. Featuring extensive technology transfers from the A350 XWB, aerodynamic improvements, cabin upgrades and 25% lower fuel burn, the A330neo is powered exclusively by Trent 7000 high-bypass turbofans, succeeding the Trent 700 used on the A330ceo. It shares a common type rating with the Airbus A350 XWB, meaning pilots can fly both aircraft interchangeably.

First deliveries of the A330-900neo, with ten additional seats, redesigned winglets and improved fuel burn, were made to TAP Air Portugal on 26 November 2018, followed in October 2020 by deliveries of the 800neo to Kuwait Airways.

Turkish Airlines, Air China and China Eastern Airlines are the largest operators of the A330 with some 68, 58 and 54 aircraft respectively (December 2019).

AIRBUS A340

The fuselage stretch on the Airbus A340-600 was achieved by inserting a 19ft 3in plug ahead of the wing and a 10ft 6in plug to the rear. G-VBLU 'Soul Sister' was flown by Virgin Atlantic for 10 years on its long-haul services that included New York-JFK, New Delhi and Lagos. She is seen here on the ramp at Hong Kong on 2 January 2012. (Ian Black)

Airbus A340

Country of origin: EU.
Type: wide-body jet airliner.
Variants: A340-200/300/500/600.
Number delivered: 377 (at January 2021), production ceased 2011.
First flight: 25 October 1991.
Entered service: 15 March 1993 with Lufthansa and Air France.
Main operators: Iberia, Lufthansa, Mahan Air, Virgin.
Powerplant: A340-200/300 – 4 × 31,200–34,000lbf CFM56-5 high-bypass turbofans; A340-500/600 – 4 × 60,000lbf Rolls-Royce Trent 500.
Performance: max speed, 570mph (M0.74, 918kmh); cruising speed, 200/300 – 541mph (M0.71, 871kmh); service ceiling, A340-200 – 41,100ft (12,527m), A340-300/500/600 – 41,450ft (12,634m); range, A340-200 – 8,000nm (14,816km), A340-300 – 7,300nm (13,520km), A340-500 – 9,000nm (16,670km), A340-600 – 7,800nm (14,450km).
Weights: max ramp weight, A340-200 – 275,000kg (606,270lb), A340-300 – 277,400kg (611,560lb), A340-500/600 – 381,200kg (840,400lb); max take-off weight, A340-200 – 275,000kg (606,270lb), A340-300 – 276,500kg (609,580lb), A340-500/600 – 380,000kg (837,760lb); max landing weight, A340-200 – 181,000kg (399,040lb), A340-300 – 192,000kg (423,290lb), A340-500 – 246,000kg (542,340lb), A340-600 – 265,000kg (584,225lb); max zero fuel weight, A340-200 – 169,000kg (372,580lb), A340-300 – 183,000kg (403,445lb), A340-500 – 232,000kg (511,470lb), A340-600 – 251,000kg (553,360lb); max fuel capacity, A340-200 – 36,678 US gals (155,040 litres), A340-300 – 39,060 US gals (147,850 litres), A340-500 – 58,875 US gals (222,850 litres), A340-600 – 54,020 US gals (204,500 litres).
Dimensions: span, A340-200/300 – 197ft 10in (60.30m), A340-500/600 – 208ft 2in (63.45m); length overall, A340-200 – 195ft 0in (59.40m), A340-300 – 208ft 11in (63.69m), A340-500 – 222ft 10in (67.93m), A340-600 – 247ft 3in (75.36m); fuselage width, A340-200/300/500/600 – 18ft 6in (5.64m); height, A340-200 – 55ft 3in (16.80m), A340-300 – 55ft 9in (16.99m), A340-500 – 56ft 8in (17.53m), A340-600 – 58ft 10in (17.93m).
Accommodation: flight crew of 2, max seating 200 – 420, typical 3-class 210–240; 300 – 440, typical 3-class 250–295; 500 – 440, typical 3-class 270–282; 600 – 475, typical 3-class 320–370.
Losses: hull losses – 6, fatalities – 0.

▼ Notable features of the Airbus A340 include a common type rating with the A330 and improved crew rest facilities, the latter an important consideration in a long-range airliner flying sectors that can be up to 18 hours' duration. This is Surinam Airways' Airbus A340-300, PZ-TCP, arriving at Schiphol Airport on 31 October 2015. (Nieuwland Photography/Shutterstock)

Notes: The super-slender Airbus A340 is one of the most graceful and elegant jetliners ever built – compare its form with that of the lugubrious A380. With its 247ft 3in-long twin-aisle wide-body fuselage, the A340-600 variant was for some time the longest airliner in service.

Designed to operate over long distances with a full passenger load, A340s flew nonstop on many of the longest commercial air routes, including Virgin's London to Shanghai and Singapore Airlines' 16,600km Singapore to New York services. The -600 was used by most airlines to augment and, in some cases replace, long-haul 747 services. As already mentioned, the A340 was developed in parallel with the A330, combining the high technology developed for the A320 with the vast experience gained from the A300 and A310. The first of the all-new ultra-long-range Airbus family to be delivered was the 295-passenger A340-300 to Air France on 26 February 1993. The initial short-fuselage A340-200 took to the air with Lufthansa on 29 January 1993.

The A340-200/300 is powered by the CFM56-5 and (in common with the -500 and -600) is fitted with a three-leg main landing gear, with one double-bogie gear under the fuselage centreline to manage the heavy maximum take-off weight (MTOW) of 276,000kg (608,000lb). Capable of carrying 210 to

▲ Virgin Atlantic's Airbus A340-600, G-VNAP, on finals to London-Heathrow on 1 August 2018. Virgin made its last scheduled flight with the A340 on 26 October 2019. (Lukas Wunderlich/Shutterstock)

250 passengers over 6,700nm the -200 is the smallest of the A340 variants, while the 208ft 11in-long -300 can seat up to 290 passengers and has a range of 7,300nm.

Airbus announced in 1997 two significantly enlarged A340 variants to carry heavier loads over even greater distances, the A340-500 and the super-stretched -600. Both variants featured a huge increase in fuel capacity (and gross weight) to give them their ranges of 9,000nm and 7,500nm, typically carrying 282 and 370 passengers respectively, and more powerful Rolls-Royce Trent 500 engines to handle their even heavier 380,000kg (840,000lb) MTOW. The -600 entered service on 1 August 2002 with Virgin Atlantic, while the -500 began revenue flights with Emirates in October 2003.

A nail in the coffin of four-engine jetliners generally, but the thirsty A340 specifically, were changes in engine design and regulations in the early 2010s that allowed Boeing to develop its rival 777 with two engines instead of four, enabling airlines to fly many routes at a fraction of the cost.

AIRBUS A350 XWB

Airbus A350-1000, G-VLUX, was delivered to Virgin Atlantic on 10 August 2019, the first of five A350s to the airline. 'Red Velvet' is pictured on a publicity shoot for Virgin above the North Wales coast on 7 September 2019. (Ian Black)

Airbus A350 XWB

Country of origin: EU.
Type: wide-body jet airliner.
Variants: A350-900/1000.
Number delivered: 422 (at April 2021).
Main users: Air France, Lufthansa.
First flight: 14 June 2013.
Entered service: 15 January 2015 with Qatar Airways.
Produced: 2010 to present.
Main operators: Cathay Pacific, Delta Air Lines, Lufthansa, Qatar Airways, Singapore Airlines.
Powerplant: 2 × 84,200–97,000lbf Rolls-Royce Trent XWB high-bypass turbofans.
Performance: max speed, 590mph (M0.77, 950kmh); cruising speed, 561mph (M0.73, 903kmh); service ceiling, A350-900 – 43,100ft (13,100m), A350-1000 – 41,450ft (12,634m); range, A350-900 – 8,100nm (15,000km); A350-1000 – 8,700nm (16,100km).
Weights: max ramp weight, A350-900 – 280,900kg (619,280lb), A350-1000 – 316,900kg (698,645lb); max take-off weight, A350-900 – 280,000kg (617,295lb), A350-1000 – 319,000kg (703,275lb);

max landing weight, A350-900 – 207,000kg (456,355lb), A350-1000 – 236,000kg (520,290lb); max zero fuel weight, A350-900 – 195,700kg (431,445lb), A350-1000 – 223,000kg (491,630); max fuel capacity, A350-900 – 37,248 US gals (141,000 litres), A350-1000 – 42,003 US gals (159,000 litres).
Dimensions: span, A350-900/1000 – 212ft 5in (64.75m); length overall, A350-900 – 219ft 2in (66.80m), A350-1000 – 242ft 1in (73.79m); fuselage width, A350-900/1000 – 19ft 7in (5.96m); height, A350-900 – 55ft 11in (17.05m), A350-1000 – 56ft 0in (17.08m).
Accommodation: flight crew of 2, A350-900 – max seating 400–420, typical 3-class 300–350; A350-1000 – 440, typical 3-class 350–410.
Losses: hull losses – 0, fatalities – 0.

▼ Aeroflot Airbus A350-900, VQ-BFY, boards passengers using air stairs at St Petersburg on 17 March 2020. Delivered to the Russian state airline a few weeks earlier on 29 February, 'P. Tchaikovsky' seats 316 passengers in a 28 business class, 24 premium economy and 264 economy configuration. (Alex Gensher/Shutterstock)

Notes: Developed in response to Boeing's 787 Dreamliner, the Airbus A350 XWB (eXtra Wide Body) is a long-range wide-body twinjet that first flew on 14 June 2013. The initial A350-900 entered service with launch customer Qatar Airways on 15 January 2015, and the stretched -1000 variant entered commercial service on the carrier's Doha–London route on 24 February 2018.

The A350 XWB benefits from the use of over 70% advanced materials in its construction, combining carbon composites (53%), titanium and modern aluminium alloys to create a lighter and more cost-efficient aircraft, while also reducing maintenance requirements. It also features new composite variable camber wings with winglets and the latest high lift devices.

Power is delivered exclusively by the latest-generation Rolls-Royce Trent XWB high-bypass turbofan, which has three thrust levels tailored to each of the three A350 variants (A350-900/900ULR/1000). When the lighter airframe structure is combined with the quieter and more efficient Trent XWB engines, the result is 25% lower operating costs, fuel burn and CO_2 emissions when compared with previous-generation aircraft.

The A350 XWB's glass cockpit includes new LCD instrument display screens, integrated modular avionics developed from the A380 and a head-up display (HUD). With typical twin-aisle 3-class seating

▲ The long-haul A350-900ULR (Ultra Long Range) can cover up to 9,700nm (18,000km) and is able to fly for more than 20 hours nonstop. Singapore Airlines connects Singapore with New York direct using the -900ULR on the world's longest commercial flight of 18 hours 45 minutes. This is Singapore Airlines' -900ULR, 9V-SGB, landing at Changi Airport on 11 February 2020. (Phuong D. Nguyen/Shutterstock)

for between 300 to 410 passengers (depending on the variant), the state-of-the-art Airspace cabin interior delivers optimised temperature and humidity control and a cabin altitude of 6,000ft, which means passengers are more likely to arrive at their destination feeling less fatigued.

The A350 XWB offers a true long-range capability of up to 8,100nm, but it can also be configured to operate both regional and ultra-long-haul routes. The A350-900ULR (Ultra Long Range) variant, carrying an additional 24,000 litres of fuel in its modified fuel system (with no additional tanks), can cover up to 9,700nm (18,000km) and is capable of flying for over 20 hours nonstop. Singapore Airlines connects Singapore with New York using its A350-900ULRs on the world's longest commercial flight of 18 hours 45 minutes.

In spring 2020 there were 321 A350 aircraft in service with 31 operators worldwide, the largest fleets being Qatar Airways (48), Singapore Airlines (41) and Cathay Pacific with 39 aircraft.

AIRBUS A380-800

Emirates Airbus A380-800, A6-EEZ, about to land at
Schiphol Airport, Netherlands, on 31 October 2015.
Emirates was the biggest customer for the A380, operating
a fleet of 115 aircraft before the COVID-19 pandemic struck.
(Nieuwland Photography/Shutterstock)

Airbus A380-800

Country of origin: EU.
Type: wide-body double-deck jet airliner.
Variants: A380-800.
Produced: 2003–21.
Number delivered: 246 (at December 2020).
First flight: 27 April 2005.
First introduced: 25 October 2007 with Singapore Airlines.
Main users: Emirates, Singapore Airlines, British Airways, Qantas, Lufthansa, Air France.
Powerplant: 4 × 74,740–80,210lbf Rolls-Royce Trent 900 or 4 × Engine Alliance GP7200 high-bypass turbofan engines.
Performance: max speed, 587mph (M0.77, 945kmh); cruising speed, 561mph (M0.73, 903kmh); service ceiling, 43,000ft (13,100m); range, 8,200nm (15,200km).

Weights: max ramp weight, 562,000kg (1,238,998lb) ; max take-off weight, 560,000kg (1,268,000lb); max landing weight, 386,000kg (850,984lb); max zero fuel weight, 361,000kg (795,869lb); max fuel capacity, 84,472 US gals (323,546 litres).
Dimensions: span, 261ft 8in (79.8m); length overall, 238ft 7in (72.72m); fuselage diameter, 23ft 5in (7.14m); height, 79ft 0in (24.09m).
Accommodation: flight crew of 2, typical passenger seating 525 in 3 classes, 853 max.
Losses: hull losses – 0, fatalities – 0.

▼ Singapore Airlines was the launch customer for the A380 in 2007. This is the carrier's 9V-SKN on the ramp at JFK on 16 June 2018, one of 24 delivered to the airline. The sorry tale is that by July 2020, two had been scrapped, nine were stored, ten parked, two were still active and one had been sold. (Ian Black)

Notes: The four-engine Airbus A380 is the world's largest passenger aircraft flying today, operating some of the world's longest commercial routes. Everything about it is big – from its enormous 261ft 8in wingspan to the incredible number of passengers it can carry – a certified maximum of 853. It is also a remarkable aircraft in many other ways, from the sheer size of the factories where it is built, to the major innovations in aerodynamics, structures and systems that have been integrated into its design.

Capable of carrying between 379 and 615 passengers in a variety of seating configurations on two decks, ranging from an 11-abreast economy section through to a private luxury three-room suite in first class, on routes of up to 8,200nm (15,200km), the A380 offers the lowest operating cost-per-seat of any large aircraft.

The flightdeck is a two-man operation and features a glass cockpit, fly-by-wire controls, advanced interactive instrument displays and flight management system. There are two engine options for the A380 – the Rolls-Royce Trent 900 and the Engine Alliance GP7200, with Emirates the only airline to operate A380 aircraft with both engine variants.

Entering service with launch customer Singapore Airlines on 25 October 2007, the A380 was soon delivering savings, burning 20% less fuel per seat-mile than the airline's Boeing 747-400 fleet. Much of

▲ The sheer size of the A380 is plain to see in this view of British Airways' A380, G-XLEJ, taking off from London-Heathrow Airport on 17 August 2018. Delivered to BA in November 2015, G-XLEJ was grounded in March 2020 at the beginning of the COVID-19 pandemic in Britain. (Jaroslaw Kilian/Shutterstock)

this saving is due to the use of composite materials in the aircraft's construction, which accounts for some 25% of the structural weight.

Emirates and Qantas introduced the A380 into use in 2008 with the inaugural routes Dubai–New York and Melbourne–Los Angeles. The 100th A380 was delivered on 14 March 2013 to Malaysian Airlines. From 2012, Airbus offered an increased-weight version of the A380 with a MTOW of 575,000kg – or 575 tonnes.

Emirates has been the biggest customer for the A380, with 115 aircraft delivered out of an order book of 123. However, when the Middle East carrier reduced its last orders for the super-jumbo in preference of the A350 XWB and A330neo, Airbus announced that production of the A380 would cease in 2021. Their decision was hastened by the massive drop in passenger air travel thanks to the COVID-19 pandemic, which has also seen a move by airlines to prematurely retire their large four-engine jets and instead follow a trend towards twinjets.

BOEING 717-200

Volotea Airlines' Boeing 717-23S, EC-MGT, climbs away from Palma de Mallorca Airport on 21 July 2018. The aircraft is configured for 125 economy-class passengers.

(Lukas Wunderlich/Shutterstock)

Boeing 717-200

Country of origin: USA.

Type: narrow-body jet airliner.

Variants: 717-200.

Produced: 1998 to 2006.

Number built: 156.

First flight: 2 September 1998.

First introduced: 12 October 1999 with AirTran Airways.

Main users: Delta Air Lines, Hawaiian Airlines, QantasLink, Volotea.

Powerplant: 2 × 18,950–21,430lbf Rolls-Royce BR700-715A1-30 turbofans.

Performance: cruising speed, 510mph (M0.66, 822kmh); service ceiling, 37,000ft (11,000m); range, 2,060nm (3,815km).

Weights: max take-off weight, 49,895kg (110,000lb); max landing weight, 45,362kg (100,000lb); max zero fuel weight, 42,638kg (94,000lb); max fuel capacity, 3,673 US gals (13,903 litres).

Dimensions: span, 93ft 4in (28.40m); length overall, 124ft 0in (37.80m); fuselage diameter, 10ft 11in (3.15m); height, 29ft 8in (9.00m).

Accommodation: flight crew of 2, typical passenger seating 106 in 2 classes, 117 in single class.

Losses: hull losses – 0, fatalities – 0.

▼ AirTran Boeing 717-2BD, N949AT, sports the Orlando Magic livery when it was photographed on 10 October 2012. In January 2000 it was one of the first of 89 Boeing 717s delivered to AirTran Airways. The last of the fleet was retired in January 2016. Like many of the airline's other redundant 717s, N949AT passed to Delta Air Lines in July 2015. (Airwim/Wikimedia Commons)

Notes: Specifically designed for the short-haul, high-frequency 100-passenger market, the twinjet Boeing 717 was based on the Douglas DC-9 and launched as the McDonnell Douglas MD-95. It was renamed the Boeing 717 after McDonnell Douglas and Boeing merged in 1997. As such, the 717 shares the same type rating as the DC-9 and MD-80.

The 717-200 underwent a rigorous flight-test programme in September 1998 and received joint certification a year later, becoming the first commercial aircraft to receive a Concurrent and Cooperative Certification from the US Federal Aviation Administration (FAA) and Europe's Joint Aviation Authorities (JAA). In October 2000, the FAA and JAA jointly certified the 717's first major upgrade to the aircraft's flight control computer and flight management system.

The single-aisle 717 can seat up to 117 passengers in a 2-3 configuration and has a range of up to 2,060nm. Unlike its DC-9/MD80/90 predecessors, McDonnell Douglas decided against aft air stairs for the MD-95/717, to reduce weight and improve fuel efficiency.

▲ **QantasLink Boeing 717-2K9, VH-NXG, waits for passengers to board at Port Hedland Airport in Western Australia, 27 April 2012. From 2020 National Jet Systems operates the 717 fleet on behalf of Qantas.** (Bahnfrend/ Wikimedia Commons)

Powered by a pair of rear-mounted Rolls-Royce BR700 turbofans, the engines were the result of a collaboration between BMW and the British aero engine builder to produce a series of powerplants for regional and corporate jets. The twin-shaft 18,950lbf BR700-715 powers the 717.

Launch customer AirTran Airways of Orlando, Florida, took delivery of the first 717 in September 1999. Delta Air Lines became the single largest operator of the 717 with a fleet of 91 aircraft in 2020. High despatch reliability, lower maintenance costs and ease of maintenance have all been attractive qualities to airlines operating short regional routes. On 23 May 2006, Boeing delivered the final two 717s to Midwest Airlines and AirTran Airways in a ceremony at their factory at Long Beach, California.

Boeing 737 family

The Boeing 737 is a single family of aircraft that comes in four generations: 1st – Original (737-100/200), 2nd – Classic (737-300/400/500), 3rd – Next Generation or NG (737-600/700/700ER/800/900/900ER) and 4th – 737 MAX (737 MAX 7/MAX 8/MAX 200/MAX 9. The first 737 entered service with Lufthansa on 10 February 1968.

► With baggage loading almost complete, Venezuelan carrier Avior's Boeing 737-400, YV-3317, is ready for pushback at Bogotá-El Dorado International Airport in Colombia on 31 January 2019. Also seen are A320-200s belonging to Avianca (N764AV) and Viva Air Colombia (HK-5051). (Markus Mainka/Shutterstock)

Boeing 737 Classic

Country of origin: USA.

Type: narrow-body jet airliner.

Variants: 737-300/400/400SF/500.

Produced: 1981 to 2000.

Number built: 1,988 (at May 2020).

First flight: 24 February 1984.

First introduced: 28 November 1984 with USAir.

Historic main users: American Airlines, All Nippon Airways, British Airways, easyJet, Ryanair, Southwest Airlines, United Airlines.

Powerplant: 2 × 22,000–23,500lbf CFM56-3B/C turbofans.

Performance: max cruise, 544mph (M0.71, 876kmh); cruising speed, 495mph (M0.65, 796kmh); service ceiling, 37,000ft (11,278m); range, 737-300 – 2,255nm (4,176km), 737-400 – 2,060nm (3,820km), 737-500 – 2,375nm (4,398km).

Weights: max take-off weight, 737-300 – 62,822kg (138,500lb), 737-400 – 68,038kg (150,000lb), 737-500 – 60,554kg (133,500lb); max landing weight, 737-300 – 51,710kg (114,021lb), 737-400 –

54,885kg (121,021lb), 737-500 – 49,895kg (110,018lb); max zero fuel weight, 737-300 – 47,625kg (105,013lb), 737-400 – 51,256kg (113,019lb), 737-500 – 46,720kg (103,018lb); max fuel capacity, 5,311 US gals (20,100 litres).

Dimensions: span, 94ft 9in (28.90m); length overall, 737-300 – 109ft 7in (33.40m), 737-400 – 119ft 7in (36.40m), 737-500 – 101ft 9in (31.00m); fuselage diameter, 12ft 4in (3.76m); height, 36ft 6in (11.10m).

Accommodation: flight crew of 2, typical passenger seating, 737-300 – 126 in 2 classes, 140 max; 737-400 – 147 in 2 classes, 159 max; 737-500 – 110 in 2 classes, 122 max.

Losses: 737-300 – hull losses – 36, fatalities – 719; 737-400 – hull losses – 24, fatalities – 237; 737-500 – hull losses – 8, fatalities – 220.

▼ Cardig Air Boeing 737-400SF, PK-DJK, is a non-Boeing freighter conversion. Here it has just taken off from runway 07L at Soekarno-Hatta International Airport, Tangerang, Indonesia, on 30 May 2020. (axell rf/Shutterstock)

Notes: The advanced technology Boeing 737-300/400/500 family of narrow-body jetliners was the second generation of the original Boeing 737-100/200. These newer jets were designed to be among the quietest and most fuel-efficient aircraft in the world. All three variants benefited from technology introduced on the Boeing 757 and 767 models, including advanced structural materials, new corrosion-inhibiting techniques, advanced digital avionics technology, improved aerodynamics including extensively redesigned wings and high-bypass CFM56 turbofan engines.

The 737-300 first flew on 24 February 1984 and entered revenue service with USAir on 28 November. The original 737-200 fuselage was stretched by adding a 44in section forward of the wing and a 60in section aft of the wing to make the -300. A further fuselage stretch added 10ft to the 737-400, which was introduced to service on 15 September 1988 with Piedmont Airlines. A non-Boeing freighter conversion, the 737-400SF, was pioneered at this time by Alaska Airlines. The 737-500 became the shortest Classic variant with a 101ft 9in-long fuselage, offered as a direct replacement of the original -200 series, entering service on 28 February 1990 with Southwest Airlines.

By 1987, the 737 was the most ordered commercial aircraft type in history. In January 1991,

▲ **Boeing 737-500, JA301K of All Nippon Airways applies reverse thrust after landing at Osaka-Itami Airport on 29 January 2018. ANA retired its last 737-500 on 14 June 2020. The -500 was nicknamed the 'Super Dolphin' because some in Japan say it resembled the cetacean in spirit. Cartoon dolphins are painted on the engine pods to serve as a reminder.** (Jeerapan Jankaew/Shutterstock)

2,887 737s were on order, and models 737-300, -400 and -500 were in full production. On 9 December 1999, the last 737 Classic, a 737-400, rolled off Boeing's assembly line at Renton, Washington, completing a production run of 1,988 aircraft – which breaks down as 1,113 737-300s, 486 737-400s and 389 737-500s.

Direct competitors of the 737 Classic on regional airline routes were the McDonnell Douglas MD-80 series and the Airbus A320 family, which led eventually to the 737 Next Generation (NG). Southwest Airlines, the world's largest operator of the 737, retired its fleet of 737-300s and -500s in 2016–17. The COVID-19 pandemic accelerated what was already an existing retirement programme for the Classic among the major airlines, with many operators replacing their 737 Classics with the 737NG and (unsurprisingly) with the Airbus A320 family. However, it continues to be used around the world, mainly in Indonesia, Bolivia and Peru.

Boeing 737 NG (Next Generation)

Country of origin: USA.

Type: narrow-body jet airliner.

Variants:
737-600/700/700ER/800/800BCF/900/900ER

Produced: 1996 to present.

Number built: 7,073 (at April 2021).

First flight: 9 February 1997.

First introduced: 17 December 1997 with Southwest Airlines.

Main users: American Airlines. Ryanair, Southwest Airlines, United Airlines.

Powerplant: 2 × 20,000–27,000lbf CFM56-7B18 turbofans.

Performance: cruising speed, 737-600 – 520mph (M0.68, 838kmh), 737-700 – 518mph (M0.68, 834kmh), 737-800 – 523mph (M0.68, 842kmh), 737-900ER – 524mph (M0.68, 844kmh); service ceiling, 41,000ft (12,497m); range, 737-600 – 3,235nm (5,991km), 737-700 – 3,010nm (5,570km), 737-800 – 2,935nm (5,436km), 737-900ER – 2,950nm (5,460km).

Weights: max take-off weight, 737-600 – 65,544kg (144,500lb), 737-700 – 70,080kg (154,500lb), 737-800 – 79,016kg (174,200lb), 737-900ER – 85,139kg (187,700lb); max landing weight, 737-600 – 55,111kg (121,500lb), 737-700 – 58,604kg (129,200lb), 737-800 – 66,361kg (146,300lb), 737-900ER – 71,350kg (157,300lb); max zero fuel weight, 737-600 – 36,378kg (80,200lb), 737-700 – 37,648kg (83,000lb), 737-800 – 41,413kg (91,300lb), 737-900ER – 44,677kg (98,495lb); max fuel capacity, 737-600/700/800 – 6,875 US gals (26,022 litres), 737-900ER – 7,837 US gals (29,666 litres).

Dimensions: span, 112ft 7in (34.32m), with winglets 117ft 5in (35.79m); length overall, 737-600 – 102ft 6in (31.24m), 737-700 – 110ft 4in (33.63m), 737-800 – 129ft 6in (39.47m), 737-900ER – 138ft 2in (42.11m); fuselage diameter, 12ft 4in (3.76); height, 41ft 3in (12.57m).

Accommodation: flight crew of 2, typical passenger seating, 737-600 – 108 in 2 classes, 123 max; 737-700 – 128 in 2 classes, 140 max; 737-800 – 160 in 2 classes, 175 max; 737-900ER – 177 in 2 classes, 177 max.

Losses: 737-600 – hull losses – 0, fatalities – 0; 737-700 – hull losses – 4, fatalities – 3; 737-800 – hull losses – 20, fatalities – 788; 737-900 – hull losses – 0, fatalities – 0.

▼ **Oman Air's CFM56-7BE-engined high-capacity long-range Boeing 737-900ER, A40-BK, was delivered to the airline on 20 May 2015. It is seen on the stand at Muscat International Airport with other Oman Air jets (A40-BAB and BAC are 737-800s) on 28 August 2019.** (LIAL/Shutterstock)

Notes: As the third-generation Boeing 737 and successor to the 737 Classic, the 737 Next Generation (NG) was launched with the 126–149-seat 737-700 in November 1993, which was delivered in December 1997 to Southwest Airlines.

Featuring a redesigned wing with new and thinner aerofoil section, thicker chord, increased span and winglets, plus redesigned vertical stabilisers, the four NG variants carry 30% more fuel and have higher MTOWs than their predecessors. They are also fitted with quieter and more fuel-efficient CFM56-7B turbofans rated at 19,500–27,300lbf at take-off. This CFM56 variant is more robust than its predecessor the CFM56-3 and offers reductions in fuel burn and maintenance costs. The NG flightdeck has also benefited from an avionics upgrade and the passenger cabin received improvements comparable to the Boeing 777.

In April 1998 the 162–189-seat 737-800 – a stretched version of the 737-700 – was delivered to launch customer Hapag-Lloyd, while in September the same year SAS received the first of the 110–132-passenger 737-600. Alaska Airlines accepted the first of the 177–189-passenger 737-900 on 15 May 2001. In 2005, customers began ordering the -900's replacement, the higher-capacity, longer-range 737-900ER, which was developed to fill

▲ **Indian carrier SpiceXpress's Boeing 737-800BCF, VT-SFF, landing at Changi International Airport on 23 July 2017. In 2015 Boeing launched a passenger-to-freighter conversion programme, with converted aircraft designated as 737-800BCF (for Boeing Converted Freighter), with the first conversions delivered in 2017.** (Corvin YO/Shutterstock)

the gap left by the 757-200 and to compete against the Airbus A321. The 737 NG makes up the greatest number of 737s flying in 2020. Ryanair is the largest operator of the 737-800 (272 aircraft), while Southwest Airlines operates a fleet of 495 -700 and 207 -800 (data correct at 31 December 2019).

A high-performance derivative of the 737-700 is the Boeing Business Jet (BBJ), which was launched in 1996 as a joint venture between Boeing and General Electric and designed for corporate and VIP uses. The BBJ 2, announced in October 1999, is based on the 737-800 and has 25% more cabin space and twice the cargo space of the BBJ.

Boeing ceased assembling the 737 NG in 2019 with the last deliveries made to KLM in December 2019 and China Eastern Airlines on 5 January 2020. However, production of the military variant, the P-8 Poseidon, continues. The third-generation 737 NG has been superseded by the fourth-generation 737, the 737 MAX.

Boeing 737 MAX

Country of origin: USA.

Type: narrow-body jet airliner.

Variants: 737 MAX 7/MAX 8/MAX 8-200/MAX 9/ MAX 10.

Produced: 2016 to present.

Number delivered: 476 (at April 2021; as of 1 January 2020 it had over 4,000 orders).

First flight: 29 January 2016.

First introduced: 22 May 2017 with Malindo Air.

Main users: WestJet, Malindo Air, Ryan Air, Lion Air.

Powerplant: 2 × 26,786–29,317lbf CFM International LEAP-1B turbofans.

Performance: max speed, 541mph (M0.71, 871kmh); cruising speed, 520mph (M0.68, 838kmh); service ceiling. 41,000ft (12,497m); range, MAX 7 – 3,850nm (7,130km), MAX 8/MAX 9 – 3,550nm (6,570km), MAX 10 – 3,300nm (6,110km).

Weights: max take-off weight, MAX 7 – 80,286kg (177,000lb), MAX 8 – 82,190kg (181,229lb), MAX 9 88,314kg (194,700lb), MAX 10 – not yet advised; max landing weight, MAX 7 – 66,043kg (145,600lb), MAX 8 – 69,309kg (152,800lb), MAX 9 – 74,344kg (163,900lb); max zero fuel weight, MAX 7 –

62,913kg (138,700lb), MAX 8 – 65,952kg (145,400lb), MAX 9 – 70,987kg (156,500lb), MAX 10 – not yet advised; max fuel capacity, 6,878 US gals (26,035 litres).

Dimensions: span, 117ft 10in (35.90m); length overall, MAX 7 – 116ft 8in (35.56m), MAX 8 – 129ft 8in (39.52m), MAX 9 – 138ft 4in (42.16m), MAX 10 – 143ft 8in (43.80m); fuselage diameter, 12ft 4in (3.76m); height, 40ft 4in (12.30m).

Accommodation: flight crew of 2, typical passenger seating, MAX 7 – 138–153 in 2 classes, 172 max; MAX 8 – 162–178 in 2 classes, 210 max; MAX 9 – 178–193 in 2 classes, 220 max; MAX 10 – 188–204 in 2 classes, 244 max.

Losses: hull losses – 2, fatalities – 346.

▼ **Pre-delivery to Lion Airlines, this unmarked Boeing 737 MAX 9 is pictured at the Boeing Company's factory at Renton, Washington, on 9 September 2018, where Boeing 737 Next Generation (NG) and 737 MAX aircraft are built. It was the fatal crash of a Lion Air 737 MAX 8 aircraft (PK-LQP) on 29 October 2018 that led to the worldwide grounding of the entire 737 MAX programme.** (Thiago B. Trevisan/Shutterstock)

Notes: The 737 MAX is the fourth generation of the Boeing 737 design, succeeding the 737 NG. It made its first flight on 29 January 2016 and commenced service with Malaysian carrier Malindo Air on 22 May 2017.

Coming in four variants the 737 MAX features more efficient CFM International LEAP-1B turbofan engines, aerodynamic and airframe modifications and split-tip winglets. At December 2019 the order book was looking very healthy with 4,932 firm orders, but following two fatal crashes involving 737 MAX aircraft operated by Lion Air (Flight 610, 29 October 2018) and Ethiopian Airlines (Flight 302, 10 March 2019), orders tumbled after the 737 MAX fleet was grounded worldwide in March 2019.

At the heart of the problem was a new automated flight control, the Maneuvering Characteristics Augmentation System (MCAS), which can repeatedly push the aircraft's nose down in flight if uncorrected. The FAA suspended the 737 MAX's airworthiness certificates and in January 2020 Boeing halted production of the MAX. Airlines cancelled orders and within months the grounding had cost Boeing

▲ **Boeing 737 MAX 8, C-FNAX, lands at Calgary International Airport, Alberta, Canada, on 21 April 2018. WestJet has a fleet of 146 Boeing 737 NG and MAX aircraft.** (Acefitt/Creative Commons)

$18.6 billion in compensation to airlines and victims' families, lost business and legal fees.

In August 2020, the FAA suggested four key design changes to the 737 MAX to address the safety issues that led to the crashes. Boeing worked closely with the FAA to resolve these and the FAA re-certified the aircraft in mid-November 2020. Airlines were slow to resume MAX operations and rollout was cautious, but by March 2021 the aircraft was flying again with 14 airlines worldwide.

Boeing intends to deliver most of its 450-aircraft stockpile of 737 MAX aircraft within a year of restarting deliveries. The company had stockpiled these aircraft because it did not stop building the MAX throughout much of 2019, even though it was unable to deliver the jets owing to the worldwide grounding. In mid-2021 production levels were still low, but Boeing hopes to be making 31 737 MAX jets a month by early 2022.

BOEING 747-400

In 2019 British Airways celebrated its centenary year by repainting four current aircraft in heritage liveries from the airline's past. Boeing 747-400, G-BYGC (seen here), was repainted in the classic BOAC livery. Golf Charlie is pictured landing at Chicago-O'Hare International Airport on 29 March 2019. (Carlos Yudica/Shutterstock)

Boeing 747-400

Country of origin: USA.

Type: wide-body jet airliner.

Variants: 747-400 (original), 400F (Freighter), 400M
(Combi), 400D (Domestic), 400ER (Extended
Range), 400ERF (Extended Range Freighter),
400BCF (Boeing Converted Freighter), 400LCF
(Large Cargo Freighter).

Produced: 1988–2009.

Number built: 694.

First flight: 29 April 1988.

First introduced: 9 February 1989 with Northwest
Airlines.

Number in service 2020: 295.

Main users 2020: Atlas Air, British Airways,
Lufthansa, Qantas, UPS Airlines,
Virgin Atlantic.

Powerplant: 747-400/400F – 4 × 56,500–
63,300lbf Pratt & Whitney PW4000/General Electric
CF6/Rolls-Royce RB211 high-bypass turbofan
engines; 747-400ER – 4 × GE CF6; 747-400ERF –
PW4000/GE CF6.

Performance: max speed, 623mph (M0.81,
1,004kmh,); cruising speed, 747-400/400ER –
579mph (M0.75, 933kmh), 747-400F/400ERF –
573mph (M0.75, 922kmh); cruise altitude 34,700ft
(10,576m); range, 747-400 – 7,285nm (13,490km),
747-400ER – 7,585nm (14,045km), 747-400F –

4,455nm (8,250km), 747-400ERF – 4,985nm
(9,230km).

Weights: operating empty weight, 747-400 –
183,523kg (404,600lb), 747-400ER – 187,016kg
(412,300lb), 747-400F – 163,701kg (360,900lb),
747-400ERF – 164,019kg (361,600lb); max take-off
weight, 747-400 – 396,893kg (875,000lb), 747-
400ER – 412,769kg (910,000lb), 747-400F –
396,893kg (875,000lb), 747-400ERF – 412,769kg
(910,000lb); max landing weight, 747-400ER –
260,360kg (574,000lb); max fuel capacity, 747-400
– 57,285 US gals (216,850 litres), 747-400ER –
63,705 US gals (241,150 litres), 747-400F/400ERF –
53,985 US gals (204,360 litres).

Dimensions: span, 211ft 5in (64.44m); length
overall, 231ft 10in (70.66m); fuselage width, 21ft 3in
(6.50m); height, 63ft 8in (19.41m).

Accommodation: flight crew of 2, 3-class seating
416, 2-class 524.

Losses: hull losses – 13, fatalities – 98.

▼ Before the COVID-19 outbreak, Taiwanese carrier China
Airlines operated a fleet of 22 Boeing 747-400 aircraft – 17
-400F dedicated freighters, four passenger variants and one
-400F/SCD (side cargo door). This is B-18211, a passenger 747-
400, on the stand at Hong Kong on 2 January 2012 looking
north towards mainland China and Guangdong. (Ian Black)

Notes: The advent of the Boeing 747, the world's first wide-body passenger jet, was one of the most significant milestones in aviation history. Nicknamed 'Jumbo Jet' to describe its huge size, the term became a shorthand for any large passenger aircraft. When the first 747 touched down at Heathrow Airport from New York on 22 January 1970, it heralded the dawn of a popular revolution in long-haul air travel.

To keep the 747 at the forefront of commercial aviation Boeing continued to develop the basic design, progressively improving the standard passenger 747 in addition to creating extended-range, high-density, combi and dedicated freighter versions.

The first significant redesign of the 747 was announced in 1985 with the -400 variant, which featured some major changes: a choice of three engine options, an improved and longer wing with winglets, a redesigned wing-to-fuselage fairing, improved engines, more rudder travel, lighter and more effective carbon wheel brakes, the stretched upper deck of the 747-300 and the glass cockpit designed for the 757 and 767, allowing two-pilot operation. It also offered an increased range of up to 7,285nm (13,490km) with 416 passengers in a 3-class configuration.

Northwest Airlines was the first operator of the -400 on 9 February 1989 while three months later on 31 May Singapore Airlines flew the first

▲ Loading freight through the nose door of an Air Bridge Cargo Boeing 747-400ERF ((VQ-BGY) at Moscow-Domodedovo International Airport in July 2011. Boeing built a total of 694 747-400s, making it the best-selling 747 variant. This included 442 of the passenger version, 61 combi, 19 domestic, 126 freighter, 6 ER, and 6 ERF. VQ-BGY passed to SkyLease Cargo as N904AR on 25 September 2014. (vaaalaa/Shutterstock)

international service using a -400 from Singapore to London. On 16–17 August a Qantas -400 made the first record-breaking nonstop England to Australia unrefuelled flight in 19 hours 52 minutes.

The 747-400 became a popular choice with airlines and passengers alike on long-haul routes and was operated by more than 50 passenger and cargo carriers worldwide. However, with the move towards twinjets like the Boeing 787 and Airbus A350 that offered better fuel and cost efficiencies, the -400 began to fall from favour in the late 2010s. COVID-19 accelerated the retirement of the 747-400 and on 17 July 2020 British Airways announced it was retiring all 31 of its -400s with immediate effect, brought forward from 2024. Virgin, Qantas and Lufthansa also announced the grounding of their 747-400 fleets.

In mid-2021, six airlines worldwide were using the 747 on scheduled passenger services, reduced from 22 before COVID. Lufthansa has since become the world's largest user of the 747, now all 747-8s.

Boeing 747-8

Country of origin: USA.

Type: wide-body jet airliner.

Variants: 747-8 Freighter, 747-8 Intercontinental, 747-8 VIP.

Produced: 2008 to present.

Number built: 141 (at November 2020).

First flight: 8 February 2010 (747-8F), 20 March 2011 (747-8I).

First introduced: 12 October 2011 with Cargolux (F – Freighter); 1 June 2012 Lufthansa (I – Intercontinental).

Number in service 2020: 137.

Main users 2020: AirBridge Cargo, Air China, Atlas Air, Brunei Government, Cargolux, Cathay Pacific Airways, Korean Air, Lufthansa, Nippon Cargo Airlines, Polar Air Cargo, Qatar Airways Cargo, Qatar Amiri Flight, Royal Flight of Oman, Saudi Arabian Airlines, Silk Way West Airlines, State of Kuwait, Turkey Government, UPS, Volga-Dnepr UK.

Powerplant: 4 × 66,500lbf General Electric GEnx-2B67 high-bypass turbofan engines.

Performance: cruising speed at 35,000ft, 747-8I – 567mph (M0.74, 914kmh), 747-8F – 562mph (M0.73, 903kmh); max range, 747-8I – 7,730nm (14,310km), 747-8F – 4,325nm (8,010km); ceiling 43,100ft (13,100m).

Weights: max take-off weight, 747-8I and 8F – 447,700kg (987,000lb); max landing weight, 747-8I – 312,100kg (688,062lb), 747-8F – 343,400kg (757,067lb); max zero fuel weight, 747-8I – 295,300kg (651,025lb), 747-8F – 329,00kg (725,321lb); max fuel capacity, 747-8I – 64,054 US gals (242,470 litres), 747-8F – 60,754 US gals (229,980 litres).

Dimensions: span, 224ft 5in (68.4m); length overall, 250ft 2in (76.3m); cabin diameter, 21ft 3in (6.49m); height, 63ft 6in (19.4m).

Accommodation: flight crew of 2, 747-8I – 467 passengers in 3-class, 524 (2-class) and 581 (single-class), max 605; 747-8F – 857.7cu m (139 tonnes) typical cargo volume capacity; 747-VIP – 8 to 100 passengers.

Losses: hull losses – 0, fatalities – 0.

▼ Lufthansa Boeing 747-8I, D-ABYH, has been with the German national airline since 27 March 2013 but was grounded in August 2020 owing to COVID-19. 'Thüringen' is pictured at Hong Kong on 16 July 2015. (Pawarin Prapukdee/Shutterstock)

Notes: Known initially as the 747 Advanced, the fourth-generation Boeing 747 is the successor to the 747-400 and was launched as the stretched 747-8 on 14 November 2005. Produced in two variants – the passenger -8I (Intercontinental) and the freighter -8F, the first 747-8 to be delivered was an -8F to Luxembourg-based freight airline Cargolux on 12 October 2011, while the first -8I began revenue service with Lufthansa on 1 June 2012, flying from Frankfurt to Washington DC. Special VIP versions of the 747-8 have also been sold to several governments and heads of state, including Qatar, Kuwait, Brunei and Saudi Arabia.

Drawing on design and technology from the Boeing 777 and 787 Dreamliner, the 747-8 is powered by four advanced dual-rotor General Electric GEnx-2B high-bypass turbofans. It is the largest version of the 747 and is 19ft longer than the 747-400, making it the longest passenger aircraft in service until the launch of the 777-9 in 2019 (length 251ft 9in). With its wider, thicker and deeper wings the 747-8 can hold 6,770 US gals (25,620 litres) more fuel than the basic 747-400.

Inside the passenger cabin the 747-8I echoes the style of the 787 Dreamliner, with the accents on soothing lighting and a sense of space. The -8I can

▲ Atlas Air Boeing 747-8F (N855GT) taking off from Anchorage-Ted Stevens International Airport, Alaska, on 19 February 2019. Note the chevrons or serrated nozzles on the GEnx high-bypass turbofans to reduce engine noise. (Arjan Veltman/Shutterstock)

carry 467 passengers in a 3-class layout at a range of up to 7,730nm (14,430km), while the freighter version (8F) has a shorter upper deck and is able to carry 137 tonnes of cargo over a distance of 4,120nm (7,630km). Subsequent changes to the 747-8's design have resulted in an increased MTOW to 472,000kg (1,041,000lb), strengthened main landing gear and an improvement in full payload range to 8,200nm (15,200km).

The 747-8F accounts for most of the 747-8 aircraft delivered (91 freighters against 47 of the passenger variant as at December 2019), owing to more interest among airlines currently for four-engine freighters than for passenger aircraft. It is the only in-production freighter with a nose door, allowing carriage of outsized cargo and faster turnround times, while its cargo hold also has temperature-controlled zones. The 747-8F has no direct competitor as the proposed Airbus A380 freighter variant never materialised.

BOEING 767

Boeing 767-300ER, N386AA, of American Airlines, takes off
from New York-JFK on 3 November 2013. In 2017 this
aircraft was converted to a freighter (767-300ERBDSF) by
the Israeli Bedek Aviation Group. Boeing and Bedek
compete directly in the freighter conversion market.

(Eliyahu Yosef Parypa/Shutterstock)

Boeing 767

Country of origin: USA.

Type: wide-body jet airliner.

Variants: 767-200/200ER, 767-300/300ER/300F, 767-400ER.

Produced: 1981 to present.

Number built: 1,213 (at April 2021).

First flight: 26 September 1981.

First introduced: 8 September 1982 to United Airlines.

Main users: All Nippon Airways, Amazon Air, Atlas Air, Delta Air Lines, DHL, FedEx, Japan Airlines, United Airlines, UPS.

Powerplant: 767-200 – 2 × 48,000–52,500lbf Pratt & Whitney JT9D/PW4000/General Electric CF6 high-bypass turbofan engines; 767-200ER/300 – 2 × 48,000–60,600lbf JT9D/PW4000/CF6/Rolls-Royce RB211; 767-300ER/F – 2 × 56,750–61,500lbf PW4000/CF6/RB211; 767-400ER – 2 × 60,600lbf CF6/PW4000.

Performance: cruising speed at 39,000ft, 528–560mph (M0.69–M0.73, 850–900kmh); max range, 767-200/300 – 3,900nm (7,200km), 767-200ER – 6,590nm (12,200km), 767-300ER/F – 5,980nm (11,070km), 767-400ER – 5,625nm (10,415km); ceiling, 43,000ft (13,100m).

Weights: max take-off weight, (767-200) 142,900kg (315,000lb), 767-200ER – 179,200kg (395,000lb), 767-300 – 158,800kg (350,000lb), 767-300ER – 186,900kg (412,000lb), 767-400ER – 204,100kg (450,000lb); max landing weight, 158,760kg (350,000lb); max zero fuel weight, 767-200 – 80,100kg (176,650lb), 767-200ER – 82,400kg (181,610lb), 767-300 – 86,100kg (189,750lb), 767-300ER/F – 90,000kg (198,440lb), 767-400ER – 103,900kg (229,000lb); max fuel capacity, (standard and ER) 16,700–24,140 US gals (63,216–91,379 litres).

Dimensions: span, 767-200/300 – 156ft 1in (48.51m), 767-400ER – 170ft 4in (51.92m); length overall, 767-200 – 159ft 2in (48.51m), 767-300 – 180ft 3in (54.94m), 767-400 – 201ft 4in (61.37m); fuselage width, 16ft 6in (5.03m); height, 17ft 9in (5.41m).

Accommodation: flight crew of 2, 767-22/200ER – 174 passengers in 3-class, 214 (2-class) and 245

▼ **Three All Nippon Airways Boeing 767-300s at Tokyo-Haneda International Airport on 27 May 2018. JA8670, in the midground, joined All Nippon in 1994 and was operated for 25 years before being withdrawn from use in 2019.**
(Leony Eka Prakasa/Shutterstock)

(single-class); 767-300/300ER/F – 3-class, 210, 2-class, 261, single-class, 290; 767-400ER – 3-class, 243, 2-class, 296, single-class, 409.

Losses: hull losses – 19, fatalities – 854.

Notes: It was on 8 September 1982 that the Boeing 767 flew its first commercial service with United Airlines Flight 1767 from Chicago to Denver. United was among four US domestic carriers that commenced operating the 767 that year – Delta, American and TWA. However, the poor financial state of the world aviation industry in the early 1980s, combined with weakening oil prices and European competition from Airbus Industrie, filled the launch of Boeing's first wide-body twinjet with a measure of uncertainty. Developed in parallel with the Boeing 757, the two designs shared design and technology, which made large savings for Boeing.

Although flight-tests had shown the 767 using about 60% as much fuel as the 727-100, which the 767 was designed to replace in part, analysts at the time predicted that Boeing's new wide-body would never top the sales of the popular 727 – and eventually they were proved correct with 1,825 orders for the 727 since 1960 against 1,190 for the 767.

The 767 was used primarily on US domestic and transcontinental flights, but by the mid-1980s it was at the forefront of the growth in twinjet flights across the North Atlantic. This was made possible by more reliable engines and recognised under ETOPS regulations (Extended-range Twin-engine Operational Performance Standards), the US FAA's safety rules

▲ Bedek Aviation Group converted this passenger Boeing 767-300ER (N1327A) to a freighter (BDSF) in 2016. The CF6-80-powered cargo jet has been operated on behalf of Amazon Prime since October 2017 by Atlas Air. It is seen here on 17 February 2020 at Stockton, California. (Sundry Photography/Shutterstock)

governing transoceanic flights by commercial aircraft with two engines. By the early 2000s the 767 was making more frequent transatlantic flights than all the other jet airliner types combined.

With a 2-3-2 seating configuration in the main cabin, the 767 came in three different fuselage lengths as well as in short- and long-range versions. In sales terms the most successful version was the 767-300ER (Extended Range) option, which entered service with American Airlines in March 1988. Its increased passenger capacity and enhanced range made it attractive to new and existing customers, with deliveries reaching 583 aircraft by November 2017. A 767-400ER version was developed and first joined Continental Airlines in September 2000, followed in November by Delta Air Lines.

A freighter version of the 767, the 300F, went into service with UPS Airlines in October 1995. With competitor FedEx, the two cargo airlines are the largest 767-300F operators with 72 and 88 aircraft respectively.

The 767 has also been developed for military use with a range of different applications extending from aerial refuelling tanker (KC-767 and KC-46), to aerial surveillance and airborne early warning and control (E-767, AWACS) platforms.

BOEING 777

British Airways Boeing 777-200, G-ZZZB, high over the North Atlantic at FL370 inbound to JFK on 5 August 2012. Joining BA on 28 March 1997, ZB was the world's second GE-powered 777. Withdrawn from service in March 2020, she was flown to St Athan in South Wales on 29 August for parting out and scrapping. (Ian Black)

Boeing 777

Country of origin: USA.

Type: wide-body jet airliner.

Variants: 777-200/200ER/200LR, 777-300/300ER, 777F.

Produced: 1994 to present.

Number built: 1,661 (at April 2021).

First flight: 12 June 1994.

First introduced: 7 June 1995 with United Airlines.

Main users: Air France, All Nippon Airways, British Airways, Cathay Pacific, Emirates, Etihad, FedEx, Qatar Airways, Singapore Airlines, United Airlines.

Powerplant: 777-200 – 2 × 77,200lbf (777-200ER 93,700lbf) Pratt & Whitney PW4000/Rolls-Royce Trent 800 high-bypass turbofan engines; 777-300 – 2 × 98,000lbf PW4000/RR Trent 800; 777-300ER – 2 × 115,300lbf General Electric GE90-115B; 777-200LR/777F – 2 × 110,000–115,300lbf GE90-110B/115B.

Performance: max speed, 587mph (M0.77, 945kmh); cruising speed, 554mph (M0.72, 892kmh)

▼ **GE90-110-B1-powered Boeing 777F, D-AALF, is operated from Schkeuditz near Leipzig by German cargo airline AeroLogic. It is seen here on 21 July 2017.** (Vytautas Kielaitis/ Shutterstock)

at 35,000ft (11,000m); max range, 777-200/200ER – 5,240nm/7,065nm (9,700km/13,080km), 777-300/300ER – 6,030nm/7,370nm (11,165km/13,649km), 777-200LR – 8,555nm (15,843km), 777F – 4,970nm (9,200km); ceiling, 43,100ft (13,100m).

Weights: max take-off weight, 777-200/200ER – 247,200kg/297,550kg (545,000lb/656,000lb), 777-300/300ER – 299,370kg/351,533kg (660,000lb/775,000lb), 777-200LR – 347,452kg (766,000lb), 777F – 347,615kg (766,800lb); max landing weight, 777-200/200ER – 201,840kg/ 213,180kg (445,000lb/470,000lb), 777-300/300ER – 237,680kg/251,290kg (524,000lb/554,000lb), 777-200LR – 223,168kg (492,000kg); max zero fuel weight, 777-200/200ER – 135,850kg/138,100kg (299,550lb/304,500lb), 777-300/300ER – 160,530kg/167,829kg (353,800lb/370,000lb), 777-200LR – 145,150kg (320,000lb), 777F –144,379kg (318,300lb); max fuel capacity, 777-200 – 31,000 US gals (117,340 litres), 777-200ER/300 – 45,220 US gals (171,171 litres), 777-300ER/200LR/777F – 47,890 US gals (181,283 litres).

Dimensions: span, 777-200/200ER/300 – 199ft 11in (60.93m), 777-300ER/200LR/777F – 212ft 7in (64.80m); length overall, 777-200/200ER – 209ft 1in (63.73m), 777-300/300ER – 242ft 4in (73.86m), 777-200LR/777F – 209ft 1in (63.73m); fuselage width, 20ft 4in (6.20m); height, 777-200/200ER – 60ft 9in (18.50m), 777-300/300ER – 60ft 8in (18.50m), 777-200LR/777F – 61ft 1in (18.60m).

Accommodation: flight crew of 2, 777-200/200ER – 305 passengers in 3-class, 313 (2-class) and 440 (single-class); 777-300/300ER – 3-class, 368/365, 2-class, 396, single-class, 550; 777-200LR/777F – 3-class, 301, 2-class, 317, single-class, 440.

Losses: hull losses – 8, fatalities – 540.

Notes: When the first Boeing 777 (or 'Triple Seven' as it is commonly known) entered revenue service with United Airlines on 7 June 1995, it represented a significant milestone for Boeing's designers. It was the first aircraft they had designed completely using 3D software and without having to build full-scale

mock-ups to confirm results. It was also the first time that Boeing had engaged in a comprehensive consultation process with eight leading airlines to agree on the new 777's basic design characteristics. The result was that it should feature a 'glass' cockpit and fly-by-wire controls, a cabin cross-section similar to the 747 with seating for up to 325 passengers and a 10% improvement on seat-mile costs when compared to the Airbus A330 and McDonnell Douglas MD-11.

The 777 is the largest twin-engine jet airliner currently in service – an accolade that was briefly held by the A330 before the 777's introduction in 1995. It was also the first Boeing jet airliner to come with ETOPS 180-minute certification on delivery, allowing United to operate twinjets on its Pacific routes for the first time. Early examples were delivered with nine-abreast 3-3-3 main cabin seating, but many operators later increased this to 3-4-3.

All three of the USA's big carriers – United, American and Delta – bought the big twin, while further afield the 777 has been very successful with many Asian airlines. It has also written the success stories of the Big Three Middle East carriers – Emirates, Etihad and Qatar – with Emirates the

▲ A fascinating bird's-eye view of Etihad Airways' Boeing 777-200LR, A6-LRB, at Los Angeles International Airport on 30 May 2016, before departure for Abu Dhabi. A 777 still holds the record for the longest nonstop flight ever by a commercial aircraft, set in 2005 when the first 777-200LR flew eastbound from Hong Kong to London covering 13,422 miles (21,600km). (Thiago B. Trevisan/Shutterstock)

world's largest operator of the 777. In 2020, Delta Air Lines retired its entire 777 fleet owing to falling demand caused by the COVID-19 pandemic, but the other two US carriers kept theirs flying. United operated a fleet of some 96 777s.

There are six versions of the 777, including a dedicated freighter (777F), but most numerous is the -300ER, which became an instant success when it first appeared in 2002. Some 820 have been delivered to airlines worldwide. The biggest operator of the 777F is FedEx with 46 aircraft in active service.

The next generation of 777s, known as the 777X, is planned for introduction in 2022. Incorporating many design concepts from the 787 Dreamliner, making greater use of composite materials, featuring folding wingtips and new GE9X engines, this latest iteration will be marketed as the 777-8 and 777-9.

BOEING 787 DREAMLINER

**Kodachrome moment – British Airways Boeing 787-9
Dreamliner on a PPE (personal protective equipment) run
at a rainy Mumbai-Chhatrapati Shivaji Maharaj
International Airport on 11 July 2020.** (Ian Black)

Boeing 787 Dreamliner

Country of origin: USA.
Type: wide-body jet airliner.
Variants: 787-8/9/10, BBJ 787.
Produced: 2009 to present.
Number built: 1,003 (at April 2021).
First flight: 15 December 2009.
First introduced: 26 October 2011 with All Nippon Airways.
Main users: All Nippon Airways, Air Canada, American Airlines, Air France, British Airways, Etihad Airways, Japan Airlines, United Airlines, Singapore Airlines.
Powerplant: 2 × 64,000lbf (787-8)/71,000lbf (787-9)/76,000lbf (787-10) General Electric GEnx-1B or Rolls-Royce Trent 1000 high-bypass turbofan engines.
Performance: max speed, 594mph (M0.77, 956kmh); cruising speed, 561mph (M0.74, 903kmh); max range, 787-8 – 7,355nm (13,620km), 787-9 – 7,635nm (14,140km), 787-10 – 6,430nm (11,910km); ceiling, 787-8/9 – 43,100ft (13,100m), 787-10 – 41,100ft (12,500m).
Weights: max take-off weight, 787-8 – 227,930kg (502,500lb), 787-9/10 – 254,011kg (560,000lb); max landing weight, 787-8 – 172,000kg (380,000lb), 787-9 – 193,000kg (425,000kg), 787-10 – 202,000kg (445,000lb); max zero fuel weight, 787-8 – 161,000kg (355,000lb),(787-9 – 181,000kg (400,000lb), 787-10 – 193,000kg (425,000lb); max fuel capacity, 787-8 – 33,340 US gals (126,206 litres), 787-9/10 – 33,384 US gals (126,372 litres).
Dimensions: span, 777-8/9/10 – 197ft 3in (60.12m); length overall, 787-8 – 186ft 1in (56.72m), (787-9) 206ft 1in (62.81m), 787-10 – 224ft 0in (68.28m); fuselage width, 18ft 11in (5.77m); height, 787-8 – 55ft 6in (16.92m), 787-9/10 – 55ft 10in (17.02m).
Accommodation: flight crew of 2, 787-8 – 242 passengers in 2-class, 359 single-class; 787-9 – 290 in 2-class, 406 in single-class; 787-10 – 2-class, 330, single-class, 440.
Losses: hull losses – 0, fatalities – 0.

▼ KLM's Boeing 787-10 Dreamliner, PH-BKA, departs Schiphol Airport on 2 July 2019. 'Orange Blossom' is painted in the special KLM '100 years' anniversary livery. (Nieuwland Photography/Shutterstock)

Notes: Embracing the latest design and materials technologies, the 787 uses composite structures which represent 50% of the aircraft by weight; advanced aerodynamics – like its variable camber wing, unique one-piece composite barrel construction that results in the elimination of all longitudinal skin splices, raked wingtips and low-drag empennage; more electric systems, including electric brakes; 'Smoother Ride Technology' that dampens out turbulence via the advanced fly-by-wire system; and next-generation engines – General Electric GEnx-1B and Rolls-Royce Trent 1000. Taken together, these improvements offer a 20% to 25% reduction in fuel and emissions over current jets such as the 767 and A330.

On the flightdeck, new technologies are applied while maintaining commonality with other Boeing aircraft, particularly the 777. The flightdeck is equipped with a full suite of navigation and communication radios and avionics, dual HUD, very large flat-panel multifunction displays, dual Electronic Flight Bags (EFB) and an electronic checklist.

Inside the cabin a huge effort has been made to increase passenger comfort. The spacious, comfortable look and feel of the cabin is enhanced by soft LED lighting; there are improvements in noise quality and vibration thanks to interior materials that reduce 'squeaks'; quieter air conditioning; changes to

▲ **Rolls-Royce Trent 1000-powered Japan Airlines Boeing 787-8, B788, takes off from Tokyo-Narita International Airport in April 2020. Note the shape of the variable camber wing and raked wingtips.** (Kenken spotter/Shutterstock)

engine inlet and fan designs that lessen the 'buzzsaw' noise and laminar flow nacelles with 'chevrons' reducing engine noise. The 787's cabin is pressurised to a new maximum level of 6,000ft – 2,000ft lower than most other commercial aircraft, which means passengers experience fewer headaches, and less dizziness and fatigue. A new filtration system also cleans the cabin air by removing contaminants that can cause dehydration, throat and eye irritation.

Entering revenue service with All Nippon Airways on 26 October 2011, early operations of the 787 suffered problems with its lithium-ion batteries, which caused a number of small fires on board. The FAA grounded all 787s in January 2013 until a solution was found to the battery issue, which was eventually resolved in April 2013. Some 70 airlines worldwide have ordered the 787, with deliveries standing at 1,003 in April 2021. The most popular of the three models available is the 787-9 with a range of 7,635nm, of which some 566 had been delivered to airlines as at April 2021. In mid-2021, All Nippon Airways and United Airlines were operating the largest fleets with 75 and 63 aircraft respectively.

MITSUBISHI (BOMBARDIER) CRJ700 SERIES

Delta Connection's Bombardier CRJ700ER, N625CA,
on the taxiway at LAX – Los Angeles International Airport –
on 20 February 2016. (Markus Mainka/Shutterstock)

Mitsubishi (Bombardier) CRJ700 series

Country of origin: Canada.
Type: narrow-body jet airliner.
Variants: CRJ700/700 NextGen, CRJ900/900 NextGen, CRJ705, and CRJ1000 NextGen.
Produced: 1999–present.
Number delivered: 924 (2021).
First flight: 27 May 1999.
First introduced: 25 October 2001 with Brit Air.
Main users: China Express, Endeavor Air, ExpressJet, GoJet, PSA Airlines, SkyWest Airlines, Mesa Airlines.
Powerplant: CRJ700 – 2 × 13,790lbf General Electric CF34-8C5B1 turbofans, CRJ900 – 2 × 14,510lbf CF34-8C5, CRJ1000 – 2 × 14,510lbf CF34-8C5A1.
Performance: max speed, 544mph (M0.72, 876kmh); cruising speed, 515mph (M0.68, 829kmh); service ceiling, 41,000ft (12,479m); range, CRJ700 – 1,378 (2,553km), CRJ900 – 1,553nm (2,876km), CRJ900 – 1,622nm (3,004km).
Weights: max take-off weight, CRJ700 – 34,019kg (75,000lb), CRJ900 – 38,330kg (84,500lb), CRJ1000 – 41,640kg (91,800lb); max landing weight, 30,390kg (67,000lb); max fuel capacity, CRJ700/900 – 19,595lb (8,888 litres), CRJ1000 – 8822kg (19,450lb).
Dimensions: span, CRJ700 – 76ft 3in (23.20m), CRJ900 – 81ft 7in (24.90m), CRJ1000 – 85ft 11in (26.20m); length overall, CRJ700 – 106ft 1in (32.30m), CRJ900 – 118ft 11in (36.20m), CRJ1000 – 128ft 5in (39.10m); fuselage diameter, 8ft 10in (2.70m); height, CRJ700 – 24ft 10in (7.57m), CRJ900 – 24ft 7in (7.50m), CRJ1000 – 24ft 6in (7.47m).
Accommodation: flight crew of 2, typical passenger seating, CRJ700 – 68–78, CRJ900 – 76–90, CRJ1000 – 97–104.
Losses: CRJ700 – hull losses – 0, fatalities – 0; CRJ900 – hull losses – 2, fatalities – 0; CRJ1000 – hull losses – 0, fatalities – 0.

▼ SAS Scandinavian Airlines Systems' CRJ900LR, EI-FPE, takes off at Stockholm-Arlanda Airport on 10 July 2018. Leased from CityJet on 21 April 2016, Papa Echo returned to the Irish carrier on 10 February 2020. (B. Forenius/Shutterstock)

Notes: With its eyes on the 60–100-seat market dominated in the early 1990s by the BAe 146, Embraer E-jets and the Fokker 70/100, Canadian company Bombardier Aerospace recognised the most cost-effective solution was to build on the proven technology of its existing CRJ100/200 series (CRJ standing for Canadair Regional Jet). The resultant CRJ700 series of larger 70- to 100-seat regional jet airliners became the CRJ700, CRJ900 and CRJ1000, featuring a longer fuselage, greater wingspan, more powerful General Electric CF34-8C engines, wing leading edge extensions and high-lift slats. For passenger comfort, the cabin floor was lowered by 2in to give more headroom while standing, as well as making the windows higher and closer to eye level.

The 70-seat CRJ700 entered revenue service with Brit Air in 2001, but Bombardier was already looking to move the design into the 60–100-seat market. The solution was to reconfigure the CRJ700 by adding fuselage plugs in front of and behind the wings and so the CRJ900 was born, making its first test-flight on 21 February 2001. To complete the series, a 100-seat model was launched on 19 February 2007, designated the CRJ1000. The

▲ Iberia Regional/Air Nostrum's Bombardier CRJ1000, EC-LOV, lifts off from Toulouse-Blagnac Airport in France on 23 October 2012. The carrier's CRJ1000s are used widely on regional flights between Spanish and French destinations. (Laurent Errera L'Union, France/Creative Commons)

CRJ700 also comes in extended-range (ER) and long-range (LR) versions.

To keep the CRJ series current, Bombardier launched its NextGen modernisation programme in 2007, which involved aerodynamic changes and cabin upgrades including larger passenger windows, more baggage space and LED lighting across all three variants. Further cabin improvements were made in 2016.

The CRJ700 series remains one of the world's most popular regional airliners. According to statistics provided by Bombardier it accounted for 20% of all jet departures in North America in 2015, where the largest operators of the CRJ700 series are located.

In the late 2000s Bombardier sold off several of its aircraft programmes, with the CRJ programme going to Japan's Mitsubishi Heavy Industries on 1 June 2020.

DE HAVILLAND CANADA DASH 8-400

Landing at Schiphol International Airport on 3 April 2016, Flybe Airlines' super-stretched de Havilland Canada Dash 8-Q402, G-JEDM, was grounded on 5 March 2020 when the airline ceased operations, one of the first to be hit financially by the sudden downturn in traffic brought about by the **COVID-19 pandemic.** (Fasttailwind/Shutterstock)

De Havilland Canada Dash 8-400

Country of origin: Canada.
Type: narrow-body turboprop airliner.
Variants: Q200/Q300/Q400.
Produced: 1983 to present.
Number built: 1,249 (2018)
First flight: 20 June 1983.
First introduced: 1984 with NorOntair.
Main users: Jazz, QantasLink, SpiceJet, Horizon Air, WestJet Encore.
Powerplant: 2 × 5,071shp Pratt & Whitney PW150 turboprops.
Performance: max cruise speed, 414mph (M0.55, 667kmh); long-range cruise speed, 345mph (M0.46, 556kmh); service ceiling, 27,000ft (8,229m); max range, 1,100nm (2,040km).

Weights: max take-off weight, 30,481kg (67,199lb); max landing weight, 29,029kg (63,997lb); max fuel capacity, 1,724 US gals (6,526 litres).
Dimensions: span, 93ft 3in (28.42m); length overall, 107ft 9in (32.80m); fuselage diameter, 8ft 10in (2.69m); height, 27ft 5in (8.34m).
Accommodation: flight crew of 2, passenger seating 82–90.
Losses: hull losses – 13, fatalities – 101.

▼ QantasLink (Sunstate Airlines) stretched Dash 8-Q315, VH-SBI, on approach to land at Melbourne International Airport on 28 September 2011. The 'Q' stands for quiet. (Ryan Fletcher/Shutterstock)

Notes: The 70-seat Dash 8 Series Q400 is the latest iteration of the successful Dash-8 family that first flew in 1983. With new and more powerful twin Pratt & Whitney PW150 turboprop engines driving six-blade propellers, improved avionic and systems, combined with a modified wing and stretched fuselage, it is virtually an all-new aircraft. The Dash 8 has become a favourite with regional airlines around the world for short-haul services, allowing operation from shorter runways than regional jets and offering better fuel consumption.

Developed from the four-engined STOL Dash 7, three 'classic' versions of the non-STOL Dash 8 were offered initially – the 37–40-seat Dash 8-100 (1984) and the more powerful Dash 8-200 (1995), the stretched Dash 8-300 with 50–56 seats in 1989, followed in 1999 by the Dash 8-400 (68–90 seats). The 400 series is the only version that remains in production in 2020. The Dash 8-Q400 entered service in 2000 featuring the ANVS (Active Noise and Vibration Suppression) system, which reduces cabin noise to levels found on jets.

In 2018 the first of the 90-seat Dash 8-Q400 NextGen were delivered to launch customer SpiceJet, featuring redesigned landing gear, reduced fuel and maintenance costs, updated cabin interiors and baggage bins. A series of company ownership changes over time has led to an identity

▲ The smallest of the Dash 8 family, the Dash 8-200 superseded the original -100 in 1995 with more powerful engines. Here, Air Greenland's Dash 8-200 makes its landing approach at Keflavik Airport in Iceland on 2 July 2017. (Markus Mainka/Shutterstock)

crisis for the Dash 8: in 1986 the Canadian Government privatised de Havilland Canada (DHC) and sold it to Boeing in 1988, which coincided with the development of the Dash 8-200 and 56-seat Dash 8-300. A stretched 400 series followed in 1998, carrying 78 passengers and offering a higher cruising speed and better range. DHC never made the money Boeing had hoped for and in 1992 it was sold to Canadian aerospace company Bombardier, who proceeded to change the Dash 8's name to the Q-series – Q100/200/300 – the 'Q' standing for quiet, offering a low noise footprint on arrival and departure. In 2009 the new owner announced that it was ceasing production of the Dash 8-100/200/300 classic series and focusing instead on the Q400. More changes came in 2019 when Bombardier divested itself of the Q series to Longview Aircraft Company of Canada's subsidiary Viking Air, reviving the de Havilland Aircraft of Canada brand. By now the wheel had turned full circle with the decision to rename what had been the Bombardier Q400 as the de Havilland Canada Dash 8-400.

EMBRAER ERJ FAMILY

American Eagle's Embraer ERJ-140LR, N847AE, powers
out of Los Angeles International Airport on 10 March 2010.
(Ryan Fletcher/Shutterstock)

Embraer ERJ family

Country of origin: Brazil.
Type: narrow-body jet airliner.
Variants: ERJ135/ERJ140/ERJ145/ERJ145XR.
First flight: 11 August 1995.
Produced: 1995 to 2020.
Number built: 1,231 (at 2020).
First introduced: 6 April 1997 with ExpressJet Airlines.
Main users: Airlink, ExpressJet, Envoy Air, Piedmont Airlines, CommutAir.
Powerplant: ERJ135/ERJ140 – 2 × 7,580lbf Rolls-Royce AE 3007-A1/3 turbofan engines, ERJ145 – 2 × 8,917lbf AE 3007-A1/E turbofan engines.
Performance: max cruise speed – 517mph (M0.78, 833kmh), ERJ145XR – 530mph (M0.80, 854kmh); ceiling 37,000ft (11,278m); range ERJ135LR – 1,750nm (3,240km), ERJ140LR – 1,650nm (3,060km), ERJ145XR – 2,000nm (3,700km); service ceiling, 37,000ft (11,278m).

Weights: max take-off weight, ERJ135 – 20,000kg (44,092lb), ERJ140 – 21,100kg (46,517lb), ERJ145 – 24,100kg (53,131lb); max fuel capacity LR (long range) version, 1,188 US gals (4,499 litres); XR (extra long-range), 1,578 US gals (5,973 litres).
Dimensions: span, 65ft 9in (20.04m); length overall, ERJ135 – 86ft 5in (26.33m), ERJ140 – 93ft 4in (28.45m), ERJ145 – 98ft 0in (29.87m); fuselage diameter, 7ft 6in (2.28m); height, 22ft 2in (6.76m).
Accommodation: flight crew of 2; ERJ135 – 37 passengers; ERJ140 – 44; ERJ145 – 50.
Losses: hull losses – 8, fatalities – 0.

▼ **Embraer ERJ135, N16525, operated by Contour Airlines, takes off from Phoenix-Sky Harbor International Airport in the United States on 8 April 2019. The ERJ family was particularly popular with the North American market, which operated 68% of the fleet as feeder aircraft linking up all the hubs of the major carriers.** (Markus Mainka/Shutterstock)

Notes: Embraer's ERJ family of twin-engine regional jets comprises the ERJ135, ERJ140 and ERJ145. The ERJ145 was first revealed to airlines in 1989, based on the company's earlier EMB120 design. It was not until 1996 that the ERJ145 with its low-mounted swept wings, T-tail and rear-mounted engines first entered service with ExpressJet Airlines in the USA (which became the largest operator of the ERJ145, with a fleet of some 270 at its peak, and the only operator of the longer-range ERJ145XR). The ERJ145 was the most numerous of the family and accounted for 78% of ERJ145s in operation.

Meeting the needs of regional airlines for a cost-effective jet for commuter and feeder routes, the ERJ145 family appealed to carriers around the world where fast turnarounds and a high daily utilisation were needed. All three baseline models of the ERJ family share 95% parts commonality and a common pilot type rating, avoiding the added cost of maintaining separate pilot pools. Bombardier's regional CRJ jet series is the main competitor for the ERJ family.

▲ Ukrainian carrier Dniproavia Airlines operated 24 ERJ-135 and -145 aircraft between 2007 and 2017 when it ceased operations. Here, Embraer ERJ145LR, UR-DNR, takes off from Moscow-Sheremetyevo International Airport on 20 July 2012. (Fasttailwind/Shutterstock)

Two shortened versions of the baseline model ERJ145 were subsequently introduced, the ERJ140 in 2001 and ERJ135 in 1999, seating 44 and 37 passengers respectively. All three variants have a digital cockpit and three-abreast 2-1 seating configuration. Of the 16 variants of the ERJ145 family only 11 are used by airlines, the remaining five being business jets and military versions.

There are several sub-variants of the ERJ145 that are specific to their operator, including the ERJ145LU, which is only operated by Luxair. The ERJ145LI, which is operated only in China, is the designator for ERJ145 aircraft assembled in China in a joint venture between Harbin Aircraft Manufacturing Corporation and Embraer. These aircraft are not for export.

EMBRAER E-JET FAMILY

Passengers disembark from a Flybe Embraer E175 jet (G-FBJA) at Cardiff Airport in June 2019. The airline is now owned by Connect Airways having been bought out of administration in 2019 by a consortium including Virgin Atlantic and Stobart Group.

(Ceri Breeze/Shutterstock)

Embraer E-Jet family

Country of origin: Brazil.
Type: narrow-body jet airliner.
Variants: E170/E175/E190/E195/E175-E2/E190-E2/E195-E2.
First flight: 19 February 2002.
Produced: 2001 to present.
Number built: 1,596 (at March 2021).
First introduced: 17 March 2004 with LOT Polish Airlines.
Main users: Aeroméxico Connect, Azul Linhas Aéreas Brasileiras, Helvetic Airways, jetBlue, KLM Cityhopper, LOT Polish Airlines, Mesa Airlines, SkyWest Airlines.
Powerplant: 2 × 14,200lbf General Electric CF34-8E (E170, E175), 2 × 20,000lbf GE CF34-10E (E190, E195) high-bypass turbofan engines.
Performance: max cruise speed, E170, E175, E190 – 541mph (M0.81, 871kmh,); ceiling, E170, E175, E190 – 41,000ft (12,500m); range, E170 – 2,150nm (3,982km), E175 – 2,200nm (4,074km), E190 – 2,450nm (4,537km).
Weights: max take-off weight, E170 – 38,600kg (85,098lb), E175 – 40,370kg (89,000lb), E190 – 51,800kg (114,199lb), E195 – 52,290kg (115,280lb);

max landing weight, E170 – 33,300kg (73,414lb), E175 – 34,100kg (75,178lb), E190 – 44,000kg (97,003kg), E195 – 45,800kg (100,972lb); max fuel capacity, E170 – 3,071 US gals (11,625 litres), E175 – 3,071 US gals (11,625 litres), E190/E195 – 4,267 US gals (16,153 litres).
Dimensions: span, E170, E175 – 85ft 4in (26.00m), E190, E195 – 94ft 3in (28.72m); length overall, E170 – 98ft 1in (29.90m), E175 – 103ft 11in (31.68m), E190 – 118ft 11in (36.24m), E195 – 126ft 10in (38.65m); fuselage diameter, 9ft 11in (3.01m); height, E170, E175 – 32ft 4in (9.85m), E190 – 34ft 8in ((10.57m), E195 – 34ft 7in (10.55m).
Accommodation: flight crew of 2; E170 – single-aisle 2-class seating 66, single-class 72; E175 – 2-class 76, single-class 78; E190 – 2-class 96, single-class 100/114; E195 – 2-class 100, single-class 116/124.
Losses: hull losses – 8, fatalities – 79.

▼ **Embraer E195LR, G-FBEG, joined Flybe in November 2007 but has been in storage since October 2019.** (Tim Felce/Creative Commons)

Notes: Brazilian aerospace manufacturer Embraer launched its E-jet family at the Paris Air Show in 1999, production began at its São José dos Campos factory in July 2000 and the prototype E170 first flew on 19 February 2002. Type certification followed in Brazil, the US and Europe in 2004.

Conceived and designed to operate on low-demand routes with 70-seat capacity, the narrow-body medium-range twin-turbofan E-jet series has grown to become popular with national and regional airlines around the world, but particularly with US regional carriers. Their quiet General Electric GE CF-34 turbofans allow E-jets to operate into smaller regional airports where noise restrictions are strict, as at London City Airport.

The family has two branches – the shorter E170/175 (66–78 passengers) and the longer E190/195 (96–146). All E-jets retain the same fuselage cross-sections and avionics and are configured with single-aisle 2-2 seating in economy and 2-1 in premium. Given the high degree of commonality between the two versions, flight crews can cross-train with ease. Each variant comes in a standard version, but they can be optioned as either LR – Long Range, or AR – Advanced Range (the latter strengthened to allow more payload to be carried over an extended range, enabling higher

▲ Embraer E190-E2, P4-KHA, was delivered to Air Astana on 1 December 2018, leased from AerCap. It is seen here wearing the stunning Snow Leopard custom livery at Kyiv-Boryspil International Airport on 14 November 2019. (Oleksandr Naumenko/Shutterstock)

take-off and landing weights), or retro-fitted to up-spec them to either the LR or AR versions. The E (Enhanced) upgrade introduced in 2014 featured redesigned winglets, engine performance improvements, new avionics and interiors, although these were a bridge to the introduction of the E2 series in 2018.

Featuring new high-aspect wings, fourth-generation fly-by-wire, enhanced avionics and Pratt & Whitney PW1000G geared turbofans (which have all combined to deliver significant improvements in fuel efficiency), the E2 series includes the E175-E2, the E190-E2 and the E195-E2 – the largest aircraft in the E-jet E2 family. Passenger capacity was increased for the E175-E2 by one row of seats and the E195-E2 by three rows, allowing the latter to carry between 120 and 146 passengers. The E190-E2 remains the same as the current E190 model.

The main competitors of the E-jet are the Bombardier CRJ series, the Airbus A220 and A318, Boeing 717 and 737-600.

MCDONNELL DOUGLAS MD-11

KLM Royal Dutch Airlines McDonnell Douglas MD-11, PH-KCA, on the stand at Amsterdam-Schiphol Airport on 23 March 2013. 'Amy Johnson' was delivered to KLM on 7 December 1993 and enjoyed 21 years with the Dutch carrier before being scrapped in 2014. (NYC Russ/Shutterstock)

McDonnell Douglas MD-11

Country of origin: USA.

Type: wide-body jet airliner.

Variants: MD-11, MD-11F/BCF.

First flight: 10 January 1990.

Produced: 1988 to 2000.

Number built: 200.

First introduced: 20 December 1990 with Finnair.

Main users: FedEx, UPS.

Powerplant: 3 × 61,500lbf General Electric CF6-80C2D1F, 3 × 62,000lbf Pratt & Whitney PW4460/62 high-bypass turbofan engines.

Performance: max cruise speed, 550–584mph (M0.83–0.88, 886–940kmh); ceiling, 43,000ft (13,100m); range, MD-11 passenger – 6,725nm (12,455km), MD-11F – 3,592nm (6,652km).

Weights: max take-off weight, 273,294kg (602,500lb); max landing weight, 195,045kg (430,000lb); operating empty weight, 128,810kg (283,975lb); max fuel capacity, 38,615 US gals (146,173 litres).

Dimensions: span, 170ft 6in (51.97m); length overall, GE – 202ft 2in (61.60m), P&W – 200ft 11in (61.24m); fuselage diameter, 19ft 9in (6.0m); height, 57ft 11in (17.65m).

Accommodation: flight crew of 2; 298 in 3-class layout, 323 in 2-class, 410 single class.

Losses: hull losses – 10, fatalities – 240.

▼ **Night loading at Toronto-Pearson cargo terminal on 2 April 2019. FedEx MD-11F, N609FE, a dedicated freighter variant, is in the foreground.** (JL Images/Shutterstock)

Notes: Developed from the DC-10, the MD-11 was produced in three different versions – passenger, combi and freighter. The prototype made its first flight on 10 January 1990 and the MD-11 was introduced to service on 20 December 1990 with Finnair. Retaining the trijet configuration of the DC-10, it featured improved GE CF6-80C2 or PW4000 turbofans, a wider wing with winglets, a stretched fuselage from 182ft 2in (55.54m) to 202ft 2in (61.6m) to accommodate 298 passengers in three classes, an enhanced range of 6,725nm (12,455km) – 1,500 miles more than the DC-10 – and an increased MTOW to 285,988kg (630,500lb).

It was not a success as a passenger airliner and when McDonnell Douglas and Boeing merged in 1997 it was decided to continue MD-11 production as a freighter only. Boeing later stopped production of the aircraft in October 2000 with the 200th airframe. Like its predecessor the DC-10, the MD-11 had several inherent design flaws that made it a difficult aircraft to handle, particularly during take-off and landing. Shortcomings in its performance for range and fuel burn did not help its popularity with airlines either – Singapore Airlines cancelled its order for 20 MD-11s and instead bought the Airbus A340.

Some aerospace commentators have said that the MD-11 was one of those aircraft that was classically ill-timed – it came at the end of the three-

▲ **McDonnell Douglas MD-11F, D-ALCN, of Lufthansa Cargo climbs out of Novosibirsk-Tolmachevo International Airport on 1 April 2019. D-ALCN was the last MD-11 built, delivered to Lufthansa on 25 January 2001 and passed to UPS in 2020 as N262UP.** (faustasyan/Shutterstock)

or four-engine era, just ahead of the real move to ETOPS with the Boeing 777.

Most airlines operating the MD-11 had retired them by the end of 2004 and replaced them with the Airbus A330 and A340, and Boeing 777. KLM operated the final passenger flight of the MD-11 on 26 October 2014 from Montreal to Amsterdam.

The early end of the production of the MD-11 and subsequent collapse of passenger aircraft values led to a new life as a freighter, and the subsequent passenger-to-freighter conversion flourished. As a result, 123 MD-11 aircraft of the 147 passenger-built MD-11s (including six Convertibles and five Combis) underwent freighter conversion at Aeronavali or SASCO (Singapore).

MD-11 freighters are well suited for many medium- to longer-haul routes that have insufficient cargo volume for using a 747-400 freighter. UPS (42 aircraft in service) and FedEx (55 aircraft in service) are the biggest operators of the MD-11F type and account for some 85% of all MD-11 converted freighters currently in service.

SUKHOI SUPERJET 100

Aeroflot Russian Airlines Sukhoi Superjet SSJ100-95B, RA-89052, is prepared for service from Moscow-Sheremetyevo International Airport on 8 September 2019, one of four international airports that serve the Russian capital. That same year, Sukhoi experienced a dramatic downturn of sales of the jet, with total deliveries since 2005 standing at only 172 aircraft (it had forecast a market for 600 aircraft by 2020). (Art Konovalov/Shutterstock)

Sukhoi Superjet 100

Country of origin: Russia.
Type: narrow-body jet airliner.
Variants: SSJ100 – RRJ-95B (Basic), RRJ-95LR-100 (Long Range).
Produced: 2007 to present.
Number built: 172 (2019).
First flight: 19 May 2008.
First introduced: 21 April 2011 with Armavia.
Main users 2020: Aeroflot, Azimuth, CityJet, Interjet, Rossiya, Yakutia, Yamal Airlines.
Powerplant: 95B – 2 × 15,400lbf PowerJet SaM146-1S17 turbofan engines; LR-100 – 16,100lbf PowerJet SaM146-1S18.
Performance: cruising speed at 40,000ft, 516mph (M0.68, 828kmh); max cruise at 40,000ft, 540mph (M0.81, 870kmh); ceiling, 41,000ft (12,500m); range, 95B – 1,645nm (3,048km), LR-100 – 2,470nm (4,578km).

Weights: max take-off weight, 95B – 45,880kg (101,150lb), LR-100 – 49,450kg (109,020lb); max landing weight, 95B/LR-100 – 41,000kg (90,390lb); max fuel capacity, 95B/LR-100 – 4,175 US gals (15,805 litres).
Dimensions: span, 91ft 2in (27.80m); length overall, 98ft 3in (29.94m); cabin diameter, 10ft 6in (3.24m); height, 33ft 9in (10.28m).
Accommodation: flight crew of 2, 87 passengers in 2-class, 108 (single-class).
Losses: hull losses – 4, fatalities – 86.

▼ Azimuth Airlines' SSJ100 RRJ-95LR, RA-89079, lands at airport Rostov-on-Don's Platov International Airport on 24 May 2019. The Superjet is built cheaply and comes with a competitive price tag, it flies well and fulfils its role as a regional jet, but it has been let down by engine supply problems, a general shortage of spares and poor manufacturer support. (Evgeniyqw/Shutterstock)

Notes: Development of a Russian Regional Jet (RRJ) began in 2000 in response to a need for a 70–80-seat regional jet with a range of between 1,900 and 2,800nm (3,000 and 4,500km). It was another eight years before the resulting Sukhoi SuperJet 100 (SSJ100) made its first flight on 19 May 2008, eventually entering commercial service on 21 April 2011 with Armenian carrier Armavia, operating its inaugural rotation from Yerevan to Moscow.

Born from the collaboration between Russian plane builder Sukhoi and Italian aerospace company Leonardo, the Sukhoi SSJ100 SuperJet is a new-generation, fly-by-wire regional jet airliner. It incorporates a considerable amount of Western technology in its design and comes in two versions – the basic SSJ100 RRJ-95B and the long-range RRJ-95LR, serving short- to medium-range routes. An earlier 78-seat SSJ100-75 version was abandoned due to a lack of market interest.

SuperJet International (SJI), builder of the SSJ100, is headquartered in Venice, Italy, and is a joint venture between Russian Sukhoi Holding (90%) and Italian Leonardo Company (10%). SJI is the international arm of Sukhoi Civil Aircraft Company (SCAC) supporting the SSJ100 programme.

Powered by two PowerJet SaM146 turbofans produced by the United Engine Corporation (UEC, a joint venture between French SNECMA and Russian NPO Saturn) the engine was specially developed

▲ Sukhoi SSJ100-95LR, RA-89048, seen taking off from Moscow-Vnukovo International Airport on 10 June 2016, is one of a fleet of ten operated by Moscow-based Gazpromavia, which flies passenger and cargo charters mainly in support of the oil and gas industry. (Media works/Shutterstock)

and built for the SuperJet 100 aircraft. The cabin has five-abreast seating in a 2-3 configuration, offering more headroom than its rivals the CRJ and E-jets, and its ambience is enhanced by state-of-the-art LED lighting.

The SSJ entered an already-crowded market with the Bombardier CRJ series and Embraer's E-jets, which has not helped manufacturer SJI secure international sales for the SuperJet. Thus, many aircraft have gone to Aeroflot as the key customer, replacing its geriatric Tu-134 and Yak-42 jets, with more going to other Russian operators such as Yamal Airlines, Azimuth and Gazpromavia. Irish carrier CityJet was the first Western airline to receive an SSJ100 on 3 June 2016, eventually operating seven aircraft before the last one was withdrawn from service in February 2020. A lack of spare parts and flaky manufacturer support has led to a serviceability crisis with many user airlines. In 2019 Mexico's Interjet had only five out of their fleet of 22 aircraft operational. It had plans to replace its SSJ100s with Airbus A220 and A320 aircraft, but the airline filed for bankruptcy in December 2020.

TUPOLEV TU-204

Powered by a pair of Aviadvigatel PS-90A turbofans, the
Tupolev Tu-204C is the dedicated cargo variant of the Boeing
757-lookalike Tu-204 and is fitted with a forward side cargo
door. DHL's Tu-204C, RA-64024, lands at Moscow-
Sheremetyevo International Airport on 25 February 2017.
(Media Works/Shutterstock)

Tupolev Tu-204

Country of origin: Russia.

Type: narrow-body jet airliner.

Variants: Tu-204-100/100B/300/300A (passenger), Tu-204C/CE (Cargo), Tu-204SM, Tu-214.

Produced: 1990 to present.

Number built: 86 (December 2019).

First flight: 2 January 1989.

First introduced: 23 February 1996 with Aeroflot.

Number in service 2019: 35.

Main users 2020: Aviastar-TU, Air Koryo, Cubana de Aviación, Rossiya.

Powerplant: Tu-204-100 – 2 × 35,274lbf Aviadvigatel PS-90A; Tu-204-120 – 2 × 42,100lbf Rolls-Royce RB211-535E4B; Tu-214/Tu-204-300 – 2 × 35,582lbf Aviadvigatel PS-90A or RR RB211-535E4B; Tu-204SM – 2 × 38,581lbf Aviadvigatel PS-90A2.

Performance: cruising speed at 39,700ft (12,100m) 500–530mph (M0.66–M0.69, 810–850kmh), max speed, 560mph (900kmh); range, Tu-204-100/Tu-214 – 2,346nm (4,300km), Tu-204-120 – 2,172nm (4,100km), Tu-204-300 – 3,128nm (5,800km), Tu-204SM – 2,260nm (4,200km); service ceiling, 39,700ft (12,100m), Tu-204SM – 40,000ft (12,200m).

Weights: max take-off weight, Tu-204-100 – 105,000kg (231,500lb), Tu-204-120 – 103,000kg (227,100lb), Tu-214 – 110,750kg (244,160lb), Tu-204-300 – 107,000kg (236,000lb), Tu-204SM – 108,000kg (238,000lb); max landing weight, Tu-204-100/120/Tu-204-300 – 88,000kg (194,000lb), Tu-214 – 93,000kg (110,750kg), Tu-204SM – 89,500kg (197,300lb); max fuel capacity, Tu-204-100/120, Tu-214 –9,430 US gals (35,700 litres), Tu-204-300 – 9,510 US gals (36,000 litres), Tu-204SM – 9,457 US gals (35,800 litres).

Dimensions: span, 137ft 2in (41.80m); length overall, Tu-204, Tu-214 – 151ft 5in (46.14m), Tu-204-300 – 131ft 10in (40.19m), Tu-204SM – 151ft 5in (46.14m); cabin width, 11ft 9in (3.57m); height, 45ft 7in (13.90m).

Accommodation: flight crew of 3 (Tu-204SM – 2), 172 passengers in 2-class, 190 single-class, 204 max (Tu-204SM).

Losses: hull losses – 3, fatalities – 5.

▼ North Korean airline Air Koryo's mainstay for its Beijing–Pyongyang service is its sole Tupolev Tu-204-100B, P-633, which can carry 222 passengers in three classes. It is one of the few North Korean passenger jets allowed to fly international routes. P-633 was formerly Red Wings Airlines RA-64046 and was acquired through a Kyrgyz shell company. (Denis Kabelev/Shutterstock)

Notes: The Boeing 757-lookalike Tupolev Tu-204 was first introduced to service on 23 February 1996 with Aeroflot and was designed to replace its predecessor the Tu-154 trijet on routes that included Vladivostok to Bangkok. It is one of the new generation of Russian aircraft featuring modern technology such as fly-by-wire, glass cockpit and a supercritical wing with winglets. Conceived and designed as a family of aircraft, the Tu-204 comes in passenger, cargo, combi and quick-change versions.

There are two engine options – the Rolls-Royce RB211 and the Russian-made Aviadvigatel PS-90A. To satisfy European and ICAO noise regulations, the RB211-535-powered Tu-204-120 variant is a quieter aircraft. Cabin configuration of the basic passenger model Tu-204-100 is for 196 passengers in two-abreast 3-3 seating in economy class and 2-2 in business. The Tu-204C is a cargo version of the original passenger Tu-204 and is fitted with a forward freight door. It is the most numerous and most used variant of the aircraft.

The shortened, longer-range variant is the Tu-204-300 carrying 166 passengers that is also known as the Tu-234. It comes in two different versions – the heavier, longer-range model at 5,000nm (9,300km), and the lighter, shorter-range version at 1,900nm (3,500km).

Aimed at meeting current and future Russian and international standards, the Tu-204SM was

▲ Russian airline group Aviastar-TU provides a VIP charter service through its subsidiary, Business Aero. It flies the long-range Tupolev Tu-204-300A equipped with a luxury cabin and a conference room for VIP passengers on route sectors of up to 9,000km. Tu-204-300A, RA-64010, is seen taxiing for take-off at Vnukovo International Airport on 13 March 2015. (Media Works/Shutterstock)

developed in 2010 with features that include new glass cockpit and flight management system and an updated passenger cabin for up to 210 passengers or 174 in a typical 2-class layout. A successful test-flight of the Tu-204SM was made on 29 December 2010, but as of 2020 no aircraft have been delivered.

With a production run of only 86 (at December 2020) the Tu-204 is a rare post-Soviet Russian aircraft. Unfortunately a combination of factors conspired against it: the collapse of the Soviet Union in 1990 soon after the prototype's first flight, lack of available cash in Russia that made many indigenous airlines decide to soldier on with older types, and when they were in the position to buy new jets they opted for Western products from Boeing and Airbus.

In 2021 only seven Tu-204s remained in use of which three were operated outside Russia by Air Koryo (North Korea) and Cubana de Aviación. The remaining four aircraft are either in the fleets of Russian state entities or with freight carriers.

Legacy types in their prime – Austrian McDonnell Douglas MD-81, OE-LDS, 'Burgenland', and Pan Am Boeing 747-121, N652PA, 'Clipper Mermaid', taxiing at London-Heathrow in March 1990. (Author)

PART TWO

LEGACY AIRLINERS

AIRBUS A300

Extended-range American Airlines Airbus A300-600R, N77080, on final approach to land at New York-JFK on 8 November 2007. This CF6-80-engined aircraft was retired from American's fleet in 2009 and was later converted to a freighter. (NYC Russ/Shutterstock)

Airbus A300

Country of origin: EU.
Type: wide-body jet airliner.
Variants: A300B1/B2/B4, A300-600/600F/600RF.
First flown: 28 October 1972.
Number built: 561, ceased 2007.
Recent service: FedEx Express, UPS Airlines, European Air Transport Leipzig.

Basic data for Airbus A300-600
Powerplant: 2 × 56,000–61,000lbf CF6-80C2 or Pratt & Whitney PW4158 high-bypass turbofans.
Span: 147ft 10in (44.84m).
Length: 177ft 5in (54.10m).
Height: 54ft 3in (16.50m).

Width: 18ft 0in (5.64m).
Max cruise: 557mph (M0.73, 897kmh).
Range: A300-600R – 4,050nm (7,500km).
Passengers: 2 crew, 247 in two classes, single-class up to max 345 passengers.
Losses: hull losses – 36, fatalities – 1,435.

▼ Air France Airbus A300B4-203, F-BVGI, was delivered to the French national airline on 24 March 1977. It was converted to a freighter in 1997 and since 2003 has flown for AeroUnion in Mexico as XA-TWQ. Golf India is pictured on the stand at London-Heathrow Airport in the late 1980s. (PRM Aviation)

Notes: Described as the aircraft that launched European plane builder Airbus in 1972, the A300B and its derivatives the A300-600 and the A310 went on to become leaders in the short- to medium-haul passenger markets. The design proved versatile, spawning a series of variants and conversions that included freighters, combis, air-to-air refuelling tankers, military and VIP transport, as well as Airbus's unique fleet of five A300-600ST Beluga outsize transports. The smaller A310 is modelled on the A300 and the latter's cross-section has also been used for the later and larger A340 and A330. Launch customer Air France flew its inaugural service with the A300B2 from Paris to London on 23 May 1974. Air India became the first non-European airline to buy the aircraft, followed by Korean Air, and from the late 1970s it found many customers with other Asian airlines. With revisions to the FAA's ETOPS rule in 1977 Airbus developed the aircraft for medium- and long-haul flights and US carriers Eastern Air Lines and Pan Am bought the A300 after seeing how much more economical it was to operate compared to the Lockheed TriStar.

The improved A300-600 carrying 267

▲ **Airbus A300B4-203F, YV562T, of Transcarga Venezuela taxies at São Paulo-Guarulhos International Airport, Brazil, in 2020. Built as a passenger A300B4 and delivered to Eastern Air Lines in 1983 as N235EA, it later saw service with several other American operators including Continental and Pan Am before it was converted to a freighter in 1998.** (Matheus Obst/ Shutterstock)

passengers up to 4,000nm (7,408km) first flew on 8 July 1983 and entered service later that year with Saudi Arabian Airlines. It featured a fully digital cockpit, higher-power CF6-80 or Pratt & Whitney PW4000 engines and a redesigned rear fuselage enabling two extra rows of seats to be accommodated. It was followed in 1988 by the increased-range A300-600R.

As a testament to the soundness and longevity of its design, in 2020 one-third of Airbus's customers still operated A300/A310 aircraft as part of a wider Airbus fleet and more than 200 of the 650 aircraft currently flying with some 80 operators will still be in service in 2025. In mid-2021, FedEx is the largest operator of the A300-600RF freighter version with 65 aircraft in its fleet, and UPS with 52.

AIRBUS A310

ULS Airlines Cargo's Airbus A310-300F, TC-VEL, began life as
a standard A310-300 in 1991 with Aeroflot before conversion
to a freighter in 2009. It is pictured at Vilnius, Lithuania, on
3 May 2020. (Karolis Kavolelis/Shutterstock)

Airbus A310

Country of origin: EU.
Type: wide-body jet airliner.
Variants: A310-200/200C/200F, A310-300/300C/300F.
First flown: 3 April 1982.
Number built: 255, ceased 2007.
Recent service: Air Transat, Lufthansa, Pan Am, Singapore Airlines.
Powerplant: 2 × 45,800–57,900lbf Pratt & Whitney JT9D-7R4/General Electric CF6-80 high-bypass turbofans (data for A310-200).
Span: 144ft 0in (43.90m).
Length: 153ft 1in (46.66m).
Height: 51ft 10in (15.80m).

Width: 18ft 6in (5.64m).
Max cruise: 554mph (M0.73, 892kmh).
Range: A310-300 – 5,150nm (9,540km).
Passengers: 2 crew, 190–230 passengers.
Losses: hull losses – 12, fatalities – 830.

▼ Ex-Emirates (A6-EKH) and Kenya Airways (5Y-KQM) Airbus A310-300 joined Canadian carrier Air Transat in 2001 as C-GSAT and is seen here taking off from Manchester International Airport on 9 November 2018. The airline prematurely retired its six-strong fleet of A310 aircraft in March 2020 due to the COVID-19 pandemic. They will eventually be replaced by the Airbus A321LR.
(ER Images/Shutterstock)

Notes: Born out of the tenth variation study of the basic A300B design, the A300B10, the A310 programme was launched on 7 July 1978 and the first prototype made its maiden flight on 3 April 1982, receiving type certification on 11 March 1983. Entering revenue service in April 1983 with Swissair, the A310 was in competition with Boeing's 767-200 that had been introduced six months before. With a choice of Pratt & Whitney JT9D or Rolls-Royce RB211-524 turbofans, and a long-range capability – A310-200 – 3,500nm, A310-300 – 5,150nm – ETOPS regulations allowed the A310 to be used on transatlantic flights. Operators of the passenger A310 included Air France, Canadian Airlines, KLM, Lufthansa, Pan Am and Singapore Airlines. The A300 and A310 shared the same fuselage cross-section, although the A310 fuselage was 24ft shorter. A greater use of composite materials in primary and secondary structures conferred weight savings, while its two-crew glass cockpit was the same flightdeck that had been incorporated into the A300-600, allowing a dual type rating to be achieved between the two aircraft. The A310 wing was a completely redesigned iteration of that used on the A300, with later production models incorporating wingtip fences

▲ **Airbus A310-200, N805PA, was delivered to Pan Am in February 1986 as one of 21 A310s ordered by the airline. It later passed to FedEx in 1995 as N420FE following freighter conversion.** (PRM Aviation)

to reduce lift-induced drag. Benefits to the passenger included a 17ft 4in-wide cabin, almost 2ft wider than its competitor the Boeing 767 at 15ft 6in, with eight-abreast seating in a 2-4-2 layout.

The A310 was not as popular or successful as its forebear the A300, with deliveries of 255 against 561. From the late 1990s it was succeeded by the more advanced Airbus A330, which led to a decrease in orders. No dedicated freighter variants of the A310 were ever built, only cargo conversions of the 200- and 300-series passenger versions. There have been no passenger variants of the A310 in service in Europe since 2018, and those that remained were cargo versions, although by 2020 many of these have been replaced by newer freighters such as the Airbus A330F. In mid-2021 some 27 A310s still remained in service, 9 with Mahan Air in Iran, 18 with various governments and private operators, and a handful of military variants with the air forces of Germany and Canada.

BOEING 707

Movie legend John Travolta's immaculate Boeing 707-138B
Qantas/Jett Clipper Johnny, N707JT, pictured on finals to land
at Paris-Le Bourget on 26 June 2007. Painstakingly restored
to how it would have looked in the 1960s when it flew
passengers on Qantas's Fiesta Route from Sydney to London,
Travolta donated the former Qantas jet to the Historical
Aircraft Restoration Society (HARS) of Australia in 2020.
(Phinalanji/Creative Commons)

Boeing 707

Country of origin: USA.
Type: narrow-body jet airliner.
Variants: 707-020 (720)/120/220/320/320B/3 20C/420.
First flown: 15 July 1954.
Number built: 865 (plus Boeing 720 – 154).
Recent service: Saha Air, ATI.
Basic data for Boeing 707-320C Intercontinental
Powerplant: 4 × 18,000lb st Pratt & Whitney JT3D-3 turbofans.

Span: 145ft 8in (44.42m).
Length: 152ft 11in (45.60m).
Height: 42ft 5in (12.94m).
Fuselage width: 12ft 4in (3.80m).
Max cruise: 600mph (M0.78, 965kmh).
Range: 3,737nm (6,920km).
Passengers: 3 or 4 crew, 189 passengers max.
Losses: Boeing 707 – hull losses – 174, fatalities – 3,039; Boeing 720 – hull losses – 23, fatalities – 256.

▼ Iran's Saha Airlines was the last civil carrier to operate a scheduled passenger service with the 707 in April 2013. This is Saha's 707-3J9C, EP-SHV, on short finals to Tehran-Mehrabad International Airport on 28 March 2011. Saha continued to make cargo flights with the 707 until they ceased in 2019. (Khashayar Talebzadeh/Creative Commons)

Notes: When Pan American World Airways made the inaugural commercial flight of the Boeing 707-120 from New York-Idlewild Airport to Paris-Le Bourget on 26 October 1958, it ushered in the exciting new era of passenger jet transport. It may not have been the word's first commercial jet airliner, for that accolade went to the de Havilland Comet, but a series of fatal crashes involving the Comet

killed the British jetliner's chances of cornering the air travel market, enabling the 707 to step in and steal the crown. Its reign lasted from 1958 until 2013, when the final scheduled passenger service was flown in Iran.

Boeing's narrow-body quad-jet rapidly became the most popular jet airliner of the 1960s and 70s. With the huge growth in mass air travel that the 707 had been instrumental in driving, Boeing's jet soon proved too small to service the massive volumes of passengers being experienced. Its design limitations meant stretching the fuselage or fitting more powerful engines were out of the question. Boeing's answer was the wide-body 747.

The Boeing 707 came in seven main variants: the 707-020 (720) was a short-fuselage short-range version with seating for 156 passengers in a single-class cabin; intended for transcontinental routes, the 189-seat 707-120 was powered by four Pratt & Whitney JT3D-3 turbofans and was the first production variant; entering revenue service in December 1959, the 707-220 was fitted with more powerful JT4A-3 turbojets for hot and high operations; with an 80-inch fuselage plug ahead of the wing, the stretched 707-320 Intercontinental offered increased range and carried up to 189

▲ Air France's Boeing 707-328 Intercontinental, F-BHSP, takes off from London-Heathrow Airport in 1972. Joining the French national carrier's fleet in 1960, 'Chateau de Villandry' was eventually scrapped in 1978. The long-range versions of the 707 were sold to nearly 50 of the world's major airlines. (clipperarctic/Creative Commons)

passengers in two classes; almost identical to the -320, the 707-420 was powered by four Rolls-Royce Conway 508 turbofans, with 37 -420s delivered to Lufthansa, BOAC, Air India, El Al and Varig between 1960 and 1963; the JT3D turbofan-powered 707-320B with aerodynamic modifications to the wing saw first service with Pan Am in June 1962, some 175 examples were built; and finally, the 707-320C was a combi (passenger-freight) version and the most numerous variant with 335 built. Military versions of the 707 include the E-3 Sentry, E-6 Mercury, and E-8 Joint STARS.

TWA flew the last scheduled service with the 707 by an American carrier in 1983, although the type remained in scheduled service with many other airlines worldwide, including in a freighter configuration. Iran's Saha Airlines became the last commercial operator of the 707 and flew the type's final scheduled passenger service in April 2013.

BOEING 727

A classic image of the American domestic jet airliner scene – a pair of Delta Airlines Boeing 727-200s (N497DA and N410DA) set against the Boston city skyline and harbour at Boston-Logan Airport, 10 July 1999. Delta and its rival American Airlines dominated the US domestic flights market in the 1990s. (QualityHD/Shutterstock)

Boeing 727

Country of origin: USA.
Type: narrow-body jet airliner.
Variants: 727-100/100C/100QC/100QF, 727-200/200C, 200 Advanced, 200F Advanced.
First flown: 9 February 1963.
Number built: 1,832, ceased August 1984.
Recent service: Iran Aseman Airlines, Kalitta Charters, 2Excel Aviation.
Basic data for Boeing 727-200
Powerplant: 3 × 14,000lbf Pratt & Whitney JT8D-7 turbofans.
Span: 108ft 0in (39.92m).
Length: 153ft 2in (49.69m).
Height: 34ft 11in (10.65m).
Width: 12ft 4in (3.80m).
Max cruise: 592mph (M0.77, 953kmh).
Range: 2,550nm (4,720km).
Passengers: 3 crew, 155 passengers max.
Losses: hull losses – 119, fatalities – 4,211.

Notes: Conceived by Boeing in the late 1950s to operate from smaller airports with shorter runways than those used by Boeing 707s, the model 727 was launched on 5 December 1960 and made its first flight on 9 February 1963, entering revenue service with US domestic carrier Eastern Air Lines on 1 February 1964.

With its characteristic T-tail and three rear-mounted engines – one each side of the fuselage and the third on top at the base of the tailfin fed through an S-duct, the single-aisle 727 typically carried 134 passengers in two classes or 155 in a single-class layout over a distance of up to 2,550

▼ Boeing 727-200, TS-JHQ, at London-Heathrow in July 1989. It was delivered new to Tunis Air in 1974 and operated with the carrier for 25 years before returning to the USA for conversion to a freighter (as N722SK). The aircraft was retired in 2017. (David Bell)

miles. The jet's popularity grew with the introduction of the larger 727-200 variant that offered seating for up to 189 passengers, and eventually 1,832 727s were built at Boeing's Renton, Washington, plant.

The 727 was the first Boeing jetliner to undergo rigorous fatigue testing, the first to have completely powered flight controls, the first to use triple-slotted flaps and the first to have an auxiliary power unit (APU). It was used extensively on domestic flights within the US and occasionally on some international flights that were within its range. The trijet's popularity also extended to operators around the world, as well as cargo and charter airlines.

After 9/11, the resulting downturn in passenger traffic, coupled with tougher restrictions on noisy old-technology low-bypass turbofan engines (like those fitted to the 727) and the cost of maintaining older aeroplanes, many airlines began to phase out

▲ The approach to Princess Juliana International Airport's single runway on the Caribbean island of Sint Maarten is over Maho Beach, making it a favourite of aviation photographers. Here, AmeriJet International's Boeing 727-200F, N395AJ, is about to touch down on Runway 10/28 on 20 September 2016. (Markus Mainka/Shutterstock)

the 727 and replace it with newer, more economical twinjets like the Boeing 737 and Airbus A320. Hush kits were fitted to many 727s to satisfy noise-control regulations at airports around the world, but many were still deemed too loud and were banned from some airports in Australia.

It was on 13 January 2019 that the 727 made its last commercial passenger flight when a 727-200 operated by Iran Aseman Airlines (EP-ASB) flew from Zahedan to Tehran. In mid-2020 a handful of 727-200s remained in use in Africa, the Americas and the UK.

BOEING 737 ORIGINAL (FIRST GENERATION)

First-Generation or Original 737 – Lufthansa's Boeing 737-200, D-ABHK, prepares to board passengers at London-Heathrow's Terminal 2 in February 1990 with a flight to Bremen. The Boeing 737 was the best-selling commercial aircraft in history with over 10,580 aircraft delivered until it was overtaken in sales by the Airbus A320 in 2019. (Author)

Boeing 737 Original (First Generation)

Country of origin: USA.
Type: narrow-body jet airliner.
Variants: 737-100, 737-200/200C.
First flown: 9 April 1967.
Number built: 1,144, ceased 1988.
Recent service: Northern Air Cargo.
Basic data for Boeing 737-200
Powerplant: 2 × 14,500–16,400lbf Pratt & Whitney JT8D-7 turbofans.
Span: 93ft (28.0m).
Length: 100ft 2in (30.53m).
Height: 37ft (11m).

Fuselage width: 12ft 4in (3.80m).
Max cruise: 544mph (M0.82, 876kmh).
Range: 2,600nm (4,800km).
Passengers: 2 crew, 130 passengers max.
Losses: hull losses – 123, fatalities – 3,269.

▼ Icaro Boeing 737-200, HC-CFL, lands at Quito-Mariscal Sucre International Airport in Ecuador on 16 June 2011. The aircraft started life on the other side of the world with British Airtours on 21 March 1980. British Airtours was set up by BA in 1969 to fulfil its charter needs for its own tour programmes. (Markus Mainka/Shutterstock)

Notes: When it was launched in 1965, Boeing's new short-range twinjet 737 faced stiff competition from the McDonnell Douglas DC-9 in the US and the BAC One-Eleven in the UK. Nicknamed the 'Baby Boeing' the 737's six-abreast seating appealed to its 17 launch customer airlines because it could carry more passengers (between 85 and 130) than its rival the five-abreast DC-9. The underwing mounting of its Pratt & Whitney JT8D low-bypass engines not only reduced cabin noise, improving passenger comfort, they also made the aircraft easier to service for maintenance teams.

To save on factory build time and bring the aircraft to market as quickly as possible, Boeing gave the 737 the same upper lobe fuselage as the 707 and 727. This allowed identical upper deck cargo pallets to be used for all three jets, while the 737 later adopted the 727's cargo convertible features enabling the interior to be switched from passenger to cargo use in the 737-200 series, which featured a 6ft 2in fuselage extension. These were the 737-200C (Combi) that allowed transition between passenger and cargo use, and the 737-200QC (Quick Change), which aided a rapid conversion between roles.

▲ Boeing 737-200F, N320DL, was delivered to freight airline Northern Air Cargo on 15 February 2015. The aircraft had spent 18 years on passenger services with Delta Air Lines before it was converted to a freighter in 2006. N320DL is seen taking off from Anchorage-Ted Stevens International Airport, Alaska, on 12 September 2018. (Thiago B. Trevisan/Shutterstock)

Like its stablemate the 727, the 737 was well suited to operating from small regional airports and from unimproved or unpaved runways. Its performance under these demanding conditions led to orders from airlines in Africa, Central and South America, Asia and Australia.

Lufthansa took delivery of the first production 737-100 model on 28 December 1967 in a ceremony at Boeing Field and the jet made its maiden revenue service on 10 February 1968. United Airlines, the first US domestic customer to order the 737, accepted the first 737-200 on 29 December 1967, entering commercial service in April 1968. Some 30 737-100s and 1,114 737-200s had been delivered by the time production ceased, with the last 737-200 delivered on 8 August 1988.

BOEING 757

DHL's Boeing 757-200PCF (Precision Conversions Freighter), G-DHKU, is a passenger-to-freighter conversion by Precision Aircraft Solutions, which offers the lowest operating empty weight and the highest payload of any 757 in production in 2020. Kilo Uniform is seen at Vilnius, Lithuania, on 4 June 2020, when the cargo carrier had 17 757-200PCFs in its fleet.

(Karolis Kavolelis/Shutterstock)

Boeing 757

Country of origin: USA.

Type: narrow-body jet airliner.

Variants: 757-200/200PF/200M/200SF/757-300.

First flown: 19 February 1982.

Number built: 1,050, ceased 2004.

Recent service: Delta Air Lines, FedEx, United Airlines, UPS Airlines.

Basic data for Boeing 757-200

Powerplant: 2 × 40,200–43,500lbf Rolls-Royce RB211-535E4(B) or 2 × 36,600–42,600lbf Pratt & Whitney PW2000-37/40/43 turbofans.

Span: 124ft 10in (38.0m).

Length: 155ft 3in (47.30m).

Height: 44ft 6in (13.60m).

Fuselage width: 12ft 4in (3.80m).

Max cruise: 570mph (M0.86, 918kmh).

Range: 3,915nm (7,250km).

Passengers: 2 crew, 239 passengers max.

Losses: hull losses – 12, fatalities – 575.

▼ Air Transat Boeing 757-23A, C-GTSE, was one of a fleet of nine 757s that operated transatlantic services between Canada and the UK during the 1990s. Sierra Echo is seen here on the stand at London-Gatwick on 1 June 1996 before departing to Vancouver, British Columbia, via Goose Bay, Newfoundland, and Calgary, Alberta. (Author)

Notes: When it entered service in 1983, the narrow-body Boeing 757 quickly proved itself to be a major improvement on its predecessor the 727 when it came to fuel economy – it was up to 80% more efficient. Carrying up to 228 passengers at ranges approaching 3,915nm (7,250km), the 757 still maintained the 727's short-field performance.

Developed in parallel with the wide-body Boeing 767, both aircraft shared the same engines, aerodynamics and build materials. The two-pilot glass cockpits of the 757 and 767 were almost identical, enabling a common type rating for pilots.

The prototype flew on 19 February 1982 and received its FAA certification on 21 December, with the first Rolls-Royce RB211-engined 757-200 flying the inaugural service with Eastern Air Lines between Atlanta and Tampa on 1 January 1983. One month later in the UK, British Airways replaced its Trident 3B jets with the 757 on the London–Belfast shuttle. The first 757 with Pratt & Whitney PW2037 engines was delivered to Delta Air Lines on 5 November 1984. By the late 1980s the 757 became a regular sight on US domestic short-haul and transcontinental services. A significant competitor on US internal flights was the MD-80, which could carry almost as many passengers as some airlines' 757s, and more cheaply. A freighter variant, the 757-200PF, entered service with UPS in September

▲ Boeing 757-236, G-CPET, wearing the retro 1983 Negus livery to mark the type's retirement from scheduled services by British Airways on 29 October 2010. The 757's final rotations were mainly between London and Madrid and Vienna. 'Stokesay Castle' is seen at London-Heathrow on 19 October 2010. (Chris Lofting/Wikimedia Commons)

1987, followed by a combi version (-200M) one year later. In 1996 the stretched 757-300 was launched with an increased MTOW, 23ft longer fuselage, wider-span wings and capable of seating up to 295 passengers in single-class configuration. It offered airlines up to 50% more cargo space as well as a 10% lower seat-mile operating cost than the -200. The 757 became a favourite in Europe with British Airways, Iberia and Icelandair, while charter carriers such as Air 2000 and LTU International used the jet for package-tour flights. ETOPS clearance was granted to PW2000-series engine 757s in 1992, opening up transatlantic services.

Production ended in 2004 when Boeing recognised that the capabilities of the latest 737s and the new 787 Dreamliner had fulfilled the market's needs. The final – and 1,050th – aircraft was delivered to Shanghai Airlines on 27 April 2005. Conversion of ex-passenger 757-200s for cargo use have given a fresh lease of life to the aircraft, with FedEx a major customer.

BOMBARDIER CRJ100/200

Bombardier CRJ200 ER is almost identical externally to the CRJ100 ER but can carry 50 passengers over 1,345nm (2,491km) at a normal cruising speed of 488mph (785kmh). RusLine's CRJ200 ER, VQ-BFB, prepares to touch down at Moscow-Vnukovo International Airport on 3 April 2019.

(Vladimir Zhupanenko/Shutterstock)

Bombardier CRJ100/200

Country of origin: Canada.
Type: narrow-body jet airliner.
Variants: CRJ100/ER/LR, CRJ200/ER/LR, CRJ200PF/SF.
First flown: 10 May 1991.
Number built: 1,008, ceased 2006.
Recent service: Comair, Delta Air Lines, Endeavor Air, ExpressJet, SkyWest Airlines.
Powerplant: 2 × 8,729lbf/9,220lbf GE CF34-3A1/3B1 high-bypass turbofans.
Span: 69ft 7in (21.21m).
Length: 87ft 10in (26.77m).
Height: 20ft 5in (6.22m).
Width: 8ft 10in (2.69m).

Max cruise: 534mph (M0.81, 860kmh).
Passengers: 2 crew, 50 passengers.
Range: CRJ200 ER – 1,345nm (1,548km).
Losses: hull losses – 19, fatalities – 165.

Notes: Developed from the Canadair Challenger 600 business jet, the Bombardier CRJ100 and CRJ200 family of single-aisle two-abreast regional airliners were formerly known as the Canadair CRJ100 and CRJ200. Canadair designed a 48-seat,

▼ SkyWest's CRJ-100ER, N594SW, arriving into Calgary International Airport in western Canada from Denver on 20 June 2019. (Heather Dunbar/Shutterstock)

19ft 5in stretched version of the Challenger to create the CRJ100, with fuselage plugs fore and aft of the reinforced and modified wing and two additional emergency exit doors.

In 1987 Canadair was sold to Bombardier and in 1989 the Canadair Regional Jet programme was launched, supported by the Canadian Government. The first of three prototype CRJ100 aircraft flew on 10 May 1991 and initial deliveries to airline customers began in late 1992, headed by launch customer Lufthansa CityLine. Extended- (ER) and long-range (LR) versions of the CRJ100 and CRJ200 were introduced, with the CRJ100 LR latter offering a 40% increase in range on the standard CRJ100. An improved version of the CRJ100, the CRJ200, was developed with more efficient General Electric CF34-3B1 high-bypass turbofan engines offering lower fuel consumption and increases in cruising speed and service ceiling.

Most CRJs have been in service in North

▲ SkyWest Airlines' Bombardier CRJ200 ER, N927SW, operated for United Airlines as a United Express carrier, stands empty of passengers and baggage after arriving at Durango-La Plata County Airport in Durango, Colorado, on 3 August 2011. (Patrick Poendl/Shutterstock)

America with the largest number operated by Utah-based SkyWest Airlines, whose 177-strong fleet (May 2020) – comprising both the CRJ100 and CRJ200 versions – flies to several hundred destinations across the USA.

Passenger-to-freighter conversions such as the CRJ100 SF, CRJ200 SF and CRJ200 PF have given a fresh lease of life to some of the older CRJs.

Bombardier ceased production of CRJ100 and CRJ200 jetliners in 2006, and in the 2010s airlines began replacing their CRJs with more modern and efficient regional jets like the Embraer E-jet and the company's CRJ700 series.

BRITISH AEROSPACE BAE 146

With clamshell airbrakes open and wing flaps lowered, WDL
Aviation's British Aerospace (BAe) 146-200, D-AMGL,
performs a characteristically steep approach into Frankfurt-
Main International Airport, Germany, on 29 April 2017.
(Vytautas Kielaitis/Shutterstock)

British Aerospace BAe 146

Country of origin: UK.
Type: narrow-body jet airliner.
Variants: BAe 146-100/200/300, Avro RJ85/100/115.
First flown: 3 September 1981.
Number built: 387, ceased 2002.
Recent service: CityJet, Airlink, Swiss Global Airlines.
Basic data for BAe 146-100
Powerplant: 4 × 6,970lbf Avco Lycoming ALF502R-5 turbofans.
Span: 86ft 4in (26.34m).
Length: 85ft 10in (26.16m).
Height: 28ft 2in (8.61m).
Cabin width: 11ft 2in (3.42m).
Max cruise: 482mph (M0.73, 776kmh).
Range: 2,090nm (3,870km).
Passengers: 2 crew, 70–82 passengers.
Losses: hull losses – 23, fatalities – 337.

Notes: With 387 aircraft produced, the Avro RJ/BAe 146 was Britain's most successful civil jet airliner programme. Hawker Siddeley Aviation's proposal for a 70–100-seat quiet aircraft for short-haul feeder routes received government support in 1973, but dire economic conditions in the UK prevented the project from going ahead until 1978.

The British Aerospace (BAe) 146 as it became known was built in three variants, the -100, -200 and -300 series. A freight-carrying variant known as the QT (Quiet Trader) was produced, along with a passenger–cargo combi model designated QC (or Quick Change). In its passenger role the 146-100

▼ Dan-Air BAe 146-100, G-BKMN, was the first of the type to enter service on 27 May 1983. It was one of seven -100 series and four -300s to fly with Dan-Air, the only UK operator of the BAe 146. It is pictured here in February 1985. (Eduard Marmet/ Airliners.net/Creative Commons)

offered a unique cabin configuration for a regional jet with a standard five-abreast layout or high-density six-abreast seating for up to 82 passengers in economy class.

Powered by four Avco Lycoming ALF502 high-bypass pylon-mounted turbofans attached underneath a high wing with full-width spoilers, a T-tail and two large clamshell airbrakes in the tail beneath the fin, the BAe 146 was designed for operation from short runways as well as in hot and high conditions. The low-noise ALF502 turbofan engines meant the jet was ideally suited to flying in and out of environmentally sensitive areas like London City Airport, earning the aircraft the nickname of the 'Whisperjet' – which was how it was marketed by BAe. A robust tricycle undercarriage with main gear positioned at the midpoint outer edges of the fuselage (such as the C-130 Hercules military transport), meant the 146 was at home using rough airstrips. In 1993 an improved version known as the Avro RJ series superseded the BAe 146 (BAe 146-100/Avro RJ70, -200/RJ85, -300/RJ100/RJ115) featuring a modernised flightdeck with EFIS and more powerful Lycoming LF507 turbofans. The first

▲ Eurowings BAe 146-300, D-AQUA, takes off from Bristol International Airport in April 2008. Uniform Alpha was first delivered to Crossair on 18 September 1991. (Adrian Pingstone/ Wikimedia Commons)

(Series 100) prototype flew on 3 September 1981 with the first production aircraft entering service with Dan-Air on 27 May 1983. Scheduled services followed from London to Berne, Toulouse, Dublin, Newcastle, Stavanger and Bergen, and from Newcastle to Amsterdam, Bristol, Cardiff and the Channel Islands. The series 200 was introduced to service on 27 June 1983 by US domestic carrier Air Wisconsin operating a high-frequency schedule linking Toledo, Fort Wayne and Appleton to Chicago-O'Hare International. Several European airlines, such as CityJet and Swiss Global Airlines, successfully operated the jet, while its short-field, long-range performance was an attraction to carriers like Lineas Aéreas Privadas Argentinas, Ansett Australia and Australian Airlines (later Qantas). Deliveries of the 122-passenger stretched -300 series began in December 1988. Several cargo airlines, including TNT, have also operated the BAe 146 QT.

DOUGLAS DC-8

Air Canada's McDonnell Douglas DC-8-63, C-FTIQ, pictured at Paris–Charles de Gaulle Airport on 17 August 1980. The following year 'IQ was converted to a freighter (63F), modified to Srs 73 standard in 1984 with CFM56 turbofans, in which year it left Air Canada. By 2017 it was registered as N803DH and flying with Skybus Jet Cargo in Peru. It was believed to be in storage in 2021. (Michel Gilliand/Wikimedia Commons)

Douglas DC-8

Country of origin: USA.
Type: narrow-body jet airliner.
Variants: DC-8 Series 10/20/30/40/50/Super 60/Super 70.
First flown: 30 May 1958.
Number built: 556.
Recent service: ATI, Skybus Jet Cargo, Trans Air Cargo Service.
Basic data for Douglas DC-6 Srs 63.
Powerplant: 4 x 17,000lb st Pratt & Whitney JT3D-1 or 18,000lb st JT3D-3 or 3B or 19,000lb st JT3D-7 turbofans.
Span: 148ft 5in (45.23m).
Length: 187ft 4in (57.12m).
Height: 42ft 5in (12.92m).
Fuselage width: 12ft 3in (3.73m).
Max cruise: 610mph (M0.80, 983kmh).
Range: 3,909nm (7,240km).
Passengers: 259.
Losses: hull losses – 83, fatalities – 2,256.

Notes: One of the classic designs of the early jet age, the DC-8 entered service simultaneously with United and Delta Air Lines on 18 September 1959, one year later than the Boeing 707. With six-abreast seating across all variants, the initial domestic model was the Srs 10, followed by the Srs 20 (improved engines), the intercontinental Srs 30, and with Rolls-Royce Conway engines the Srs 40, all with seating for 177 passengers. The short-fuselage Srs 50 was developed from the Srs 30 and came along in 1961. The passenger/cargo variant of the Srs 50 with side-loading freight door in the forward

▼ African International Airways' DC-8-62H(F), ZS-OZV, descends into Chiang Mai International Airport, Thailand, on 25 May 2008. Built in 1968 as a Srs 62H with an increased take-off weight of 158,760kg (350,000lb), the aircraft was converted to a freighter in 1995. 'OZV was sold to South African operator Stars Away International in 2009 and was believed to be in storage in 2020. (nitinut380/Shutterstock)

fuselage was called the Jet Trader and entered service in 1963.

Its lack of flexibility in meeting the needs of different airlines because of its fixed passenger capacity, fuselage length and wingspan was also a factor when compared to the different variants of the 707 on offer. Because of the DC-8's later entry into the jet airliner market, its sales trailed behind those of its rival the Boeing 707 – with 556 built against the 707/720's 1,019 – although it was still purchased by most of the world's major airlines.

To try and regain the sales initiative, in 1965 Douglas decided to offer three new models of the DC-8 known as the Super 60 Series, presenting differing permutations of fuselage stretch and payload/range performance. These were the Srs 61 with a 36ft 8in longer fuselage to accommodate up to 259 passengers; the very long range Srs 62 with aerodynamic refinements, extra fuel and a 6ft 8in stretch for up to 189 passengers; and the Srs 63 combining the best of the Srs 61 and Srs 62 to give flexibility of operation over medium to long ranges. All three versions entered airline service in 1967 and

▲ From the early 1980s, US air freight carrier Air Transport International (ATI) operated a fleet of pure cargo and combi DC-8 freighters, retiring the last examples in 2016 when Boeing 757 and 767s replaced them. This is ATI's DC-8-62CF Combi, N71CX, about to touch down at Stuttgart Airport on 14 March 2016. ATI's Srs 62CF had a 32-seat aft cabin separated from the forward cargo section by a fixed smoke barrier and 9g bulkhead. (Mike Fuchslocher/Shutterstock)

offered the greatest passenger-carrying capacity until the arrival of the Boeing 747 in 1970.

Douglas also offered combi (CF) and all-freight (AF) versions of the Super 60 with a forward cargo door, as used in the Jet Trader.

In 1982 the Super 70 Series was certificated in which the Srs 61, 62 and 63 were converted to take the more efficient CFM56-2 high-bypass turbofans with new nacelles and pylons. The Super 70s were designated DC-8-71, 72 and 73 and when introduced they were the world's quietest quad-jet airliners.

In 2020 a handful of DC-8s still remained in revenue service as freighters, with operators that included Trans Air Cargo Service in the Congo and Skybus Jet Cargo in Peru.

DORNIER 328/FAIRCHILD DORNIER 328JET

SkyWork Airlines' Dornier 328-110, HN-AEO, arrives at Berlin-Tegel International Airport on 17 August 2014. The Do 328-110 has increased MTOW and extended range compared to the standard 328-100. (Art Konovalov/Shutterstock)

Dornier 328/Fairchild Dornier 328JET

Country of origin: Germany.

Type: narrow-body turboprop/jet airliner.

Variants: Dornier 328-100/110/120/130, Fairchild Dornier 328JET.

First flown: Dornier 328 – 6 December 1991, 328JET – 20 January 1998.

Number built: Dornier 328 – 217, ceased 2000; 328JET – 111, ceased 2002.

Recent service: Dornier 328 – Sun-Air (British Airways), 328JET – Sun-Air (British Airways), Ultimate Air Shuttle, Key Lime Air.

Data for Dornier 328-110/328JET

Powerplant: 2 × 2,179hp Pratt & Whitney Canada PW119B turboprops; 2 × 6,050lbf Pratt & Whitney Canada PW306B turbofans.

Span: 68ft 10in (20.98m).

Length: 69ft 8in (21.23m).

Height: Dornier 328 – 23ft 2in (7.05m), 328JET – 23ft 9in (7.24m).

Cabin width: 7ft 4in (2.24m).

Max cruise: Dornier 328 – 390mph (M0.51, 620kmh), 328JET – 470mph (M0.62, 756kmh).

Passengers: 2 crew, 30–33 passengers.

Losses: Dornier 328 – hull losses – 6, fatalities – 4; 328JET – hull losses – 3, fatalities – 0.

Notes: Originally conceived and built by Dornier as a twin-turboprop commuter airliner for short-haul trips, the Dornier 328 made its first flight on 6 December 1991 and entered airline service on 13 October 1993 with launch customer Air Engiadina of Switzerland.

The Do 328 featured a two-crew glass cockpit and came with a possible six different cabin configurations for passenger (either in 32-seat airliner layout or in executive fit with 12 VIP seats), cargo and combi operations. Featuring a supercritical wing design for optimum cruise and climb, the airframe also made extensive use of composites that conferred significant weight savings on its structure.

Beginning with the basic 328-100, the Do 328-110 followed with increased MTOW and extended range, the Do 328-120 with improved STOL performance and the Do 328-130 with improved rudder authority at increased airspeeds. The

▼ British Airways Dornier 328JET-310, OY-NCM, operated by Danish carrier Sun-Air of Scandinavia is showcased at Istanbul Air Show held at Istanbul-Ataturk Airport on 8 October 2016. (Evren Kalinbacak/Shutterstock)

Do 328 proved particularly popular on scheduled passenger services in the USA by a number of regional airlines including Atlantic Coast Jet, Air Wisconsin, Horizon Air, Lone Star Airlines and Mountain Air Express.

The Fairchild Dornier 328JET pioneered a new class of airliner, the 30-seat regional jet giving a fresh lease of life to the Dornier 328 turboprop design. Designed in response to customer demands for a cost-efficient regional jet, the 328JET was conceived as a minimum-change development of the 328 turboprop, enabling the manufacturer to bring the aircraft to market quickly. First deliveries were in July 1999 but poor sales of the 328JET pushed Fairchild Dornier into insolvency in 2002.

Danish regional airline Sun-Air became the

▲ Bandung, Indonesia, 22 April 2017 – Xpress Air's Dornier 328-110, PK-TXM, tucks up its gear as it takes off from Husein Sastranegara International Airport. It is one of six 328-100s operated by Xpress Air, a small domestic airline offering direct flights to eastern Indonesia connecting Jakarta to 24 domestic destinations. (Jeffry Surianto/Shutterstock)

largest operator of the 328JET in the 2010s, operating scheduled services as a franchise of British Airways from its base at Billund to Brussels, Düsseldorf, Friedrichshafen, London City, Manchester, Oslo and Toulouse.

Most Do 328s and 328JETs had been retired from service by 2020, although a handful remained in use with the US Air Force and some regional airlines in Europe and the USA.

FOKKER 70/100

Rolls-Royce Tay-engined Fokker 100, OE-LVO, taxies at Warsaw in June 2016. 'Chisinau' was sold to Australian carrier Alliance Airlines as VH-UQD in October 2017 as part of Austrian Airlines' fleet modernisation with Embraer E195 aircraft. (Renatas Repcinskas/Shutterstock)

Fokker 70/100

Country of origin: Netherlands.
Type: narrow-body jet airliner.
Variants: Fokker 70/100.
First flown: Fokker 100 – 30 November 1986, Fokker 70 – 4 April 1993.
Number built: Fokker 100 – 283, Fokker 70 – 48. Both ceased in 1997.
Recent service: Alliance Airlines, Iran Aseman Airlines, QantasLink, Virgin Australia.
Powerplant: Fokker 100 – 2 × 13,850–15,100lbf Rolls-Royce Tay Mk 620-15 turbofans; Fokker 70 – 2 × 13,850lbf Rolls-Royce Tay 620 turbofans.
Span: 92ft 2in (28.08m).
Length: Fokker 100 – 116ft 7in (35.53m), Fokker 70 – 101ft 5in (30.91m).
Height: Fokker 100 – 27ft 11in (8.50m), Fokker 70 – 28ft 10in (8.50m).

Cabin width: 10ft 2in (3.10m).
Max cruise: 525mph (M0.69, 845kmh).
Range: Fokker 100 – 1,710nm (3,170km), Fokker 70 – 1,841nm (3,410km).
Passengers: Fokker 100 – crew 2, 97–122 passengers, Fokker 70 – crew 2, 72–85 passengers.
Losses: Fokker 100 – hull losses – 18, fatalities – 195; Fokker 70 – hull losses – 0, fatalities – 0.

▼ Austrian Airlines Fokker 70 (OE-LFK) and Air-Berlin Airbus A319 (D-ABGC) taxi to runway 23L at Düsseldorf International Airport, 22 September 2010. Tyrolean Airways operated regional flights on behalf of Austrian Airlines from 2003 to 2012 using the brand 'Austrian Arrows'. (Dennis Kartenkaemper/Shutterstock)

Notes: When it was introduced in February 1988 to launch customer Swissair, the twinjet Rolls-Royce Tay-powered Fokker 100 cornered the market in the 100-seat short-range regional jet class, with further orders coming from American Airlines, TAM Transportes Aéreos Regionais, USAir and British Midland. Developed from the Fokker F28 Fellowship with more economical Rolls-Royce Tay engines, the Fokker 100 kept the T-tail and rear-mounted engines of its predecessor but introduced a revised wing design with wider span, EFIS glass cockpit and redesigned cabin interior, with the most obvious external difference being its stretched fuselage, which was 18ft 8in (5.74m) longer than the F28.

Other variants of the basic design included an extended-range (ER) version introduced in 1993 with higher gross weight; the Fokker 100QC (Quick Change) airliner/freighter (1994) with a large forward freight door; and the luxury Fokker 100EJ (Executive Jet), with customised luxury interiors and seating for between 19 and 31 passengers, introduced in 2003.

When a growing number of comparable airliners such as the Airbus A320 family and Embraer E-190 became available during the 1990s, sales and prospects for the Fokker 100 took a hit. When Fokker encountered financial difficulties, it was acquired by Deutsche Aerospace AG (DASA), which in turn faced money problems that compromised its

▲ **Air Panama Fokker 100, HP-1764PST, was acquired from French airline Regional CAE on 11 June 2012. The airline offers scheduled regional flights to destinations inside Panama, and to Costa Rica and Colombia. HP-1764PST is pictured taking off from Cartagena-Rafael Núñez International Airport in Colombia.** (Markus Mainka/Shutterstock)

ability to support regional airliner programmes. In 1997, Fokker 100 production was halted after 283 aircraft had been delivered.

Swissair dropped the Fokker 100 from its fleet in 1995 after giving away many of its regional routes to Crossair, while American Airlines retired its 74-strong fleet in 2004. Many other airlines followed suit after the recession in the 2010s, replacing their Fokker 100s with newer types that offered lower operating costs. In mid-2020 there were still some 120 aircraft in service worldwide, many in Australia with Alliance Airlines, Virgin Australia Regional Airlines and QantasLink (Network Aviation).

The Fokker 100 was the basis for the shorter Fokker 70, which first flew on 4 April 1993. Indonesian launch customers Sempati Air and Pelita Air received their first Fokker 70s in March 1995, followed by British Midland and Mesa Airlines (the only F70 operator in the USA). Only 47 aircraft were built, with some 39 aircraft remaining in service in mid-2020.

MCDONNELL DOUGLAS DC-9

Delivered in 1970 to Swissair as HB-IBP, DC-9-30, XA-UDC,
was operated from 2005 until 2008 by low-cost airline
Aero California from La Paz, Baja California Sur, Mexico.
Delta Charlie is seen here after landing at Mexico City on
18 November 2005. (Mislik/Shutterstock)

McDonnell Douglas DC-9

Country of origin: USA.
Type: narrow-body jet airliner.
Variants: DC-9 Series 10/20/30/40/50.
First flown: 25 February 1965.
Number built: 976, ceased in 1982.
Recent service: Delta Air Lines, Northwest Airlines, USA Jet Airlines.
Powerplant: 2 × Pratt & Whitney JT8D.
Data for DC-9-30
Span: 93ft 3½in (28.44m).
Length: 119ft 3½in (36.36m).
Height: 27ft 9in (8.50m).
Fuselage width: 10ft 9½in (3.34m).
Max cruise: 557mph (M0.73, 897kmh).
Range: 1,500nm (2,800km).
Passengers: flight crew of 2, 115 passengers max.
Losses: hull losses – 145, fatalities – 3,697.

Notes: Conceived for short-range flights after the introduction of the company's large four-engine DC-8 in 1959, the smaller DC-9 went on to become the mainstay of US domestic airlines operating short-haul internal flights. With single-aisle five-abreast coach seating for between 90 and 115 passengers (depending on the variant), the T-tailed DC-9 was powered by a pair of rear-mounted Pratt & Whitney JT8D turbofans.

The first of the Douglas DC-9 family was the Series 10, which was flown on 25 February 1965

▼McDonnell Douglas DC-9-33F, N327US, operated by cargo carrier USA Jet Airlines, at Detroit-Willow Run Airport, Michigan, 9 September 2003. Since 1969 this freighter has served with SAS and Evergreen International before passing to USA Jet in 2000. (Dmitry Avdeev/Creative Commons)

and entered commercial service on 29 November 1965 with Delta Air Lines. It was followed by the inaugural flights of the Series 30 on 1 August 1966, Series 40 (28 November 1967), Series 20 (18 September 1968) and the first Series 50 to fly and enter service in 1975.

The original DC-9 Series 10 had a plain wing, while all later versions had leading edge slats and extended wingtips. The Series 30 came in four main sub-variants: the DC-9-31 (passenger); Series 32 freighter in four sub-variants (-32LWF – Light Weight Freight; -32CF – Convertible Freighter; -32AF – all-freight); Series 33 (passenger/cargo or all-cargo); Series 34, passenger and CF version. A choice of engines with different thrust levels was offered for each sub-variant.

Entering service with launch customer Scandinavian Airlines System (SAS) in March 1968, the DC-9-40 with its 6ft 6in longer fuselage could seat up to 125 passengers, while the DC-9-50 followed in August 1974 when Eastern Air Lines

▲ Republic Airlines took delivery of DC-9-10, N8906E, in July 1979. The jet had already been a workhorse with Eastern Air Lines, who had received it new from McDonnell Douglas's Long Beach factory in July 1966. Eight years with Southern Airways from 1971 to 1979 preceded its arrival with Republic. It is seen here in August 1984. (Aero Icarus/Creative Commons)

introduced the largest of the DC-9 variants with a further stretch to the fuselage of 8ft 2in (2.49m), more powerful JT8D-15 or -17 engines and increased capacity for 135 passengers. The DC-9 was followed in 1980 by the MD-80 series.

With the steep increase in fuel prices in 2008, many operators began retiring their DC-9s and replacing them with aircraft from the Airbus A320 family, Embraer E-jets, Bombardier C-series and the Boeing 737NG. The last of the big airlines to retire their DC-9s was Delta in January 2014, although a handful of the aircraft remain in use with some smaller operators in 2020.

MCDONNELL DOUGLAS MD-80 SERIES

American's polished aluminium livery, also known as the 'tri-color' design, has been a favourite among customers and employees since it was introduced in the late 1960s. The livery was created by Massimo Vignelli, who is also known for his work on the well-known New York City Subway map. Here, McDonnell Douglas MD-82, N70401, is parked on the gate at Chicago-O'Hare International Airport on 8 August 2009.
(vaaalaa/Shutterstock)

McDonnell Douglas MD-80 series

Country of origin: USA.

Type: narrow-body jet airliner.

Variants: MD-81/82/83/87/88.

First flown: 18 October 1979.

Number built: 1,191, ceased in 1999.

Recent service: American, Delta Air Lines and Allegiant Air.

Powerplant: 2 × 18,500–21,000lbf Pratt & Whitney JT8D-200 low-bypass turbofans.

Data for MD-81/82/83/88

Span: 107ft 8in (32.82m).

Length: 147ft 10in (45.06m).

Height: 29ft 7in (9.02m).

Fuselage width: 10ft 11½in (3.34m).

Max cruise: 542mph (M0.72, 873kmh).

Range: MD-81 – 1,800nm (3,300km), MD-82 – 2,050nm (3,800km), MD-83/88 – 2,550nm (4,720km).

Passengers: flight crew of 2, 172 passengers max.

Losses: hull losses – 35, fatalities – 1,446.

Notes: Known affectionately as the 'Mad Dog' after its manufacturer's initials, the McDonnell Douglas MD-80 series was the backbone of US domestic airline fleets for more than 30 years until the COVID-19 pandemic in 2020 forced its premature retirement. 'Mad Dogs' operated across much of Delta Air Lines' domestic network and have been workhorses for the airline.

Developed from the Douglas DC-9-50 and originally known as the DC-9 Series 80, the single-aisle design was intended for frequent, short-haul flights carrying between 130 and 172 passengers, depending on the variant. The series included a stretched fuselage, a pair of rear-mounted low-

▼ Showing off the slender single-aisle fuselage and low-set swept wings of the MD-80 series, low-cost airline One-Two-Go's MD-82, HS-OME, departs Chiang Mai International Airport to Bangkok-Don Muang Airport, Thailand, on 10 October 2007. (nitinut80/Shutterstock)

bypass Pratt & Whitney JT8D-200 turbofans, small and efficient wings and a T-tail and a longer range than the DC-9.

The longer-fuselage variants – MD-81/82/83 and 88 – are 147ft 10in in length (45.06m) and capable of seating 155 passengers in five-abreast coach and with a range of up to 2,550nm. The MD-87 variant is actually 17ft (5.30m) shorter and carries 130 passengers in economy, with a range of up to 2,900nm. A freighter conversion of the MD-80 series, the MD80SF, flew in 2012, with delivery of the first aircraft to Everts Air Cargo in February 2013.

The initial flight of the DC-9 Series 80 was made on 18 October 1979 and the first aircraft were delivered to launch customer Swissair on 13 September 1980. The MD-80 series, as it became known, went on to become an export success for McDonnell Douglas with sales around the world to major airlines, including China Northern Airlines and Scandinavian Airlines System. US carrier American

▲ When the MD-88 first came out in 1988 it was an instant hit with Delta Air Lines. N908DE joined Delta in November 1992 and spent a busy 28 years with the airline as one of its 120-strong fleet of MD-88s before it was grounded in June 2020. Here, N908DE takes off from Raleigh-Durham International Airport, North Carolina, on 12 August 2018. (William Howard/Shutterstock)

Airlines was a big customer and at its peak in 2002 it had more than 360 MDs in its fleet. When the MD-88 first came out in 1988, it boasted Boeing 727-200 capacity with two instead of three engines and a lower cost per seat-mile than the Boeing 737-300, which made it a favourite with Delta Air Lines.

Although in 2018 there were 345 MD-80 Series still in service, they were rapidly being phased out by major US airlines such as American, Delta and Allegiant Air in favour of the more efficient Airbus A319/A320/A321 and Boeing 737NG. The COVID-19 pandemic led to Delta retiring its MD-88 and MD-90 fleets in June 2020.

MCDONNELL DOUGLAS MD-90

Delta was launch customer for the stretched MD-90-30 in 1995. This is Delta's MD-90-30ER, N918DH, taxiing at Hartsfield-Jackson Atlanta International Airport on 2 May 2013. (Aeroprints.com/Wikimedia Commons)

McDonnell Douglas MD-90

Country of origin: USA.
Type: narrow-body jet airliner.
Variants: MD-90-10/20/30/30EFD.
First flown: 22 February 1993.
Number built: 116, ceased in 2000.
Recent service: Delta Air Lines, Saudi Arabian
Airlines, Japan Airlines, Scandinavian Airlines.
Powerplant: 2 × 25,000lbf IAE V2525-D5 high-
bypass turbofans.
Span: 107ft 8in (32.86m).
Length: 152ft 6in (46.51m).
Height: 30ft 6in (9.33m).
Fuselage width: 10ft 11½in (3.34m).
Max cruise: 505mph (M0.66, 812kmh) at 34,777ft
(10,600m).
Range: MD-90-30 – 2,045nm (3,787km).
Passengers: flight crew of 2, 153–172 passengers.
Losses: hull losses – 3, fatalities – 1.

Notes: US carrier Delta Air Lines was the launch
customer for the MD-90, which was developed
from the MD-80 series. Following its maiden flight
on 22 February 1993, the first production aircraft
were delivered to Delta in 1995. The MD-90
featured an EFIS cockpit, a 4ft 8in (1.34m) stretch
on the basic MD-80 fuselage, and was powered by
quieter, more powerful and fuel-efficient
International Aero Engines IAE V2500 high-bypass
turbofans (the same powerplant used on the
Airbus A320ceo), making it the first variant of the
DC-9 family to use a high-bypass engine.

▼ BritishJet was a short-lived low-cost airline operating a
single MD-90-30 (HB-JIB) between Malta and the UK from
2005 to 2008. It is seen taking off from Runway 32 at Luqa on
8 June 2007. (InsectWorld/Shutterstock)

There are two versions of the MD-90 – the MD-90-30 with a range of 2,045nm (3,787km), and the MD-90-30ER, which has an increased gross weight and a range of up to 2,455nm. Depending on the cabin layout, typical seating ranges from 153 to 172 passengers. An Enhanced Flight Deck (EFD) variant of the MD-90 was built for Saudi Arabian Airlines, with a cockpit similar to the MD-11 that was also operated by the carrier.

Other main users included EVA Air, Japan Airlines, Saudi Arabian Airlines and Scandinavian Airlines. After the Boeing–McDonnell Douglas merger in 1997, Delta cancelled its remaining order for 19 MD-90s in favour of the Boeing 737-800. By 2020, however, Delta was the sole operator of the

▲ **Finnish carrier Blue1's MD-90-30, OH-BLC, was one of seven MD-90s operated on European services mainly from its base at Helsinki. Blue1 was a subsidiary of the SAS Group and merged with CityJet in 2016. It is seen at London-Heathrow on 28 July 2008.** (Chris Lofting/Wikimedia Commons)

MD-90 and flew the type's final commercial flight on 2 June.

When production of the MD-90 ceased at Long Beach in 2000, 116 airframes had been built, making production of the MD-90 the smallest of the DC-9 family. The MD was further developed into the MD-95, which was renamed the Boeing 717-200 after the two companies merged, entering service in 1999 (see page 44).

MCDONNELL DOUGLAS MD-10

FedEx MD-10-10F, N395FE, arrives at San Diego International Airport on 1 May 2013.
(Ryan Fletcher/Shutterstock)

McDonnell Douglas MD-10

Country of origin: USA.
Type: wide-body freighter conversion.
Variants: MD-10-10F/30F.
First flown: 1996.
Produced: 1997 onwards.
Recent service: FedEx, Continental, Gemini Air Cargo.
Powerplant: 3 × 40,000–50,000lbf General Electric CF6-6D/50C high-bypass turbofans.
Span: MD-10-10F – 155ft 4in (47.35m), MD-10-30F – 165ft 4in (50.39m).
Length: MD-10-10F – 182ft 3in (55.55m), MD-10-30F – 181ft 7in (55.35m).

Height: MD-10-10F – 57ft 6in (17.53m), MD-10-30F – 57ft 7in (17.55m).
Max cruise: 544mph (M0.71, 876kmh).
Range: MD-10-10F – 1,740nm (3,218km), MD-10-30F – 3,130nm (5,792km).
Max payload: MD-10-10F, 58,967kg (130,000lb), and MD-10-30F, 77,110kg (170,000lb).
Losses: hull losses – no data, fatalities – no data.

▼ DC-10-30, S2-ACR, of Biman Bangladesh Airlines, pictured at London-Heathrow in July 1989. Delivered to Biman in 1988, S2-ACR flew the last scheduled DC-10 service for the carrier on 20 February 2014. The jet was broken up at Dhaka in 2015. (David Bell)

Notes: Strictly speaking the MD-10 is not a production line aircraft. It is a conversion of the retired passenger DC-10-10 and -30 to make it functionally identical to an MD-11. At the request of FedEx, Boeing updated the older DC-10 design (under its Boeing Converted Freighter programme) to achieve compatibility with the cargo carrier's MD-11 fleet by completely replacing the cockpit with a Honeywell VIA 2000 EFIS 'glass' flightdeck. This enabled use of a common pool of pilots to operate both the MD-10 and MD-11, doing away with the flight engineer position.

The conversion programme began in 1997 and took about 120 days per aircraft. First deliveries to launch customer FedEx took place in 2000. It included a heavy maintenance check, standardisation and reliability upgrades and removal of passenger accommodation. Other main conversion activities included the 12ft × 8ft 6in main deck cargo door installation (which is common to the MD-11 freighter) on the left side of the forward fuselage, rigid cargo barrier installation to replace the standard cargo net, structural changes to increase maximum take-off gross weight (MTOGW)

▲ Avient's DC-10-30CF, Z-ARL, is the convertible cargo/passenger transport combi variant of the 30 series. It is seen at Luqa, Malta, on 12 October 2006, taking off from Runway 32. (InsectWorld/Shutterstock)

to 202,305kg (DC-10-10) and 263,086kg (DC-10-30), with a payload of 65,019kg and 81,720kg respectively for a nonstop range of approximately 2,000nm and 3,700nm.

The MD-10 programme offered by Boeing provided operators of DC-10s with a number of benefits, including lower operating costs, greater reliability, a reduced spares inventory and increased payload and range. Operators could choose a passenger-to-freighter reconfiguration, a retrofit of the DC-10 flightdeck with the advanced common flightdeck or both for maximum benefit.

FedEx has been the main operator of the MD-10 on short- and medium-haul freight routes using one MD-10-10F and 13 MD-10-30F aircraft (as at May 2021). It plans to retire them during 2021, replacing them with the Boeing 767-300ERF, Boeing 777F and the McDonnell Douglas MD-11F.

TUPOLEV TU-154

Tupolev Tu-154M, RA-85625, operated by Gazpromavia,
rotates off the runway at Vnukovo International Airport on
15 December 2014. (Media Works/Shutterstock)

Ilyushin Il-62

Country of origin: Soviet Russia.
Type: narrow-body jet airliner.
Variants: Il-62/62M/62MF.
First flown: 3 January 1963.
Number built: 292, ceased 1995.
Recent service: Aeroflot, LOT, Cubana de Aviación.
Powerplant: 4 × 24,300lbf Soloviev D-30KU turbofans.
Span: 141ft 9in (43.20m).
Length: 174ft 3in (53.12m).
Height: 40ft 6in (12.35m).
Fuselage width: 12ft 3½in (3.75m).
Max cruise: 560mph (M0.73, 900kmh).
Range: Il-62M – 5,400nm (10,000km).
Passengers: crew 3 to 5, 168–186 passengers.
Losses: hull losses – 25, fatalities – 1,086.

Notes: The Ilyushin Il-62 was the Soviet Union's first long-range jet airliner developed specifically for commercial use and was the only civil aircraft other than the British Vickers VC-10 to feature four rear-mounted engines. When it first flew on 3 January 1963 it was the world's largest jet airliner. It was also a first for several other reasons – it was the first Soviet pressurised aircraft with non-circular fuselage cross-section as well as being the first with six-abreast passenger seating.

With more than a passing resemblance to the

▼ Aeroflot Ilyushin Il-62M, CCCP-86533, on the stand at Frankfurt-Main Airport on 20 August 1983. The aircraft was withdrawn from use in 2008. (Ralf Manteufel/Wikimedia Commons)

VC-10, the similarity is only skin deep as the T-tail Il-62 was a bigger aircraft – a length of 174ft 3in against the standard VC-10's 158ft 8in, and a MTOW of 165,000kg against 142,430kg. It was also designed to operate from metalled runways at established airports whereas the VC-10 could operate from hot and high up-country airports in Africa, as used by carrier East African Airways.

The development phase of the Il-62 was a protracted affair following the first flight of the prototype in 1963, suffering with underpowered engines and requiring a wing redesign. The final production version, the basic Il-62, was powered by four 23,150lbf Kuznetsov NK8 turbofans and could carry a crew of five and 186 passengers in a single-class layout. It entered service with Aeroflot on the Moscow–Khabarovsk route on 10 March 1967, while a route-proving flight from Moscow to Montreal was flown on 11 July with a full service commencing on 15 September. A Moscow–New York service was launched on 15 July 1968, with refuelling stops at Shannon and Gander.

An improved version, the Il-62M with more

▲ Seen here at Vladivostok on 8 October 2018, P-885 is one of a pair of Ilyushin Il-62Ms operated by North Korean state airline, Air Koryo, which is the last operator of the passenger variant. P-885 was built in 1979. Note the retractable tail stand to prevent the aircraft tipping up on its tail during loading and unloading. (Denis Kabelev/Shutterstock)

powerful 24,300lbf Soloviev D-30KU turbofans, a revised flightdeck, modified wing spoilers and containerised baggage system, was introduced on 9 March 1974 and remained a mainstay of Aeroflot's long-haul fleet until well into the 1990s. It also featured increased fuel capacity giving a range of up to 5,400nm (10,000km), which did away with one of the intermediate refuelling stops when operating routes like Moscow–Washington (begun on 5 April 1974).

The Il-62 was also used by Russian client state airlines LOT, Interflug and Cubana de Aviación. Aeroflot operated a fleet of more than 180 Il-62s before retiring the type on 1 November 2001. Two examples of the Il-62MF freighter are still in use in 2020 with Belarus cargo carrier Rada Airlines.

Tupolev Tu-134

Country of origin: Soviet Russia.
Type: narrow-body jet airliner.
Variants: Tu-134/134A.
First flown: 29 July 1963.
Number built: 854, ceased 1989.
Recent service: Aeroflot, Air Koryo.
Powerplant: 2 × 14,990lbf Soloviev D-30-II turbofans.
Span: 95ft 2in (29.01m).
Length: 121ft 9in (37.10m).
Height: 29ft 7in (9.02m).
Max cruise: 550mph (M0.72, 885kmh).
Passengers: 3–5 crew, 72–84 passengers.
Losses: hull losses – 75, fatalities – 1,472.

Notes: Tupolev Design Bureau's Tu-134 was one of the most important jet airliner types to come out of the former Soviet Union, servicing Aeroflot's domestic routes. The prototype Tu-134 first flew in 1963 followed by five pre-production aircraft, before full manufacture began in 1966. Based on a similar fuselage to its forerunner, the Tu-124, the Tu-134

▼ Tu-134A-3, RA-65726, is one of three operated by Kosmos Airlines, the airline of the Russian Space Agency. Kosmos has its own dedicated terminal at Kaluga (Grabtsevo) International Airport (where this photograph was taken on 27 April 2019) for flights to Baikonur Cosmodrome in southern Kazakhstan. (Dentorson/Shutterstock)

differed by having a rear-engined layout and T-tail configuration. It replaced Tu-124 on the assembly line in the factory at Kharkov and following a series of route-proving flights within the Soviet Union with Aeroflot, it entered international revenue service in September 1967. Passenger seating was in a four-abreast layout and varied from 50 seats in the earlier model Tu-134, to 84 in the Tu-134A and 96 seats in the Tu-134B.

Like other Soviet designs of the period, the Tu-134 featured some unusual features such as wings with a sharp sweepback of 35 degrees, landing gear with low-pressure tyres for operation on unprepared runways and brake parachutes (the engines had no thrust reversers). Earlier-build Tu-134s had the distinctive glazed nose containing the navigator's position, which was done away with in later production examples. The most likely explanation for its adoption initially was for dual use by Tu-16-trained bomber crews converting to the Tu-134. A second – and major – version, the Tu-134A, was introduced in 1970 and featured a fuselage lengthened by 6ft 11in (2.11m), engine thrust reversers and improved radio and navigation equipment.

▲ Tupolev Tu-134A-3, RA-65978, of Sirius Aero landing at Vnukovo International Airport on 5 September 2014. Over the years Tupolev improved the Tu-134, expanding its load capacity and equipping it with an APU, more powerful and economical engines and thrust reversers that dispensed with the brake parachute. (Media Works/Shutterstock)

The Tu-134 was the first Soviet jet airliner to see widespread use with airlines other than Aeroflot, with operators that included CSA, Interflug, Balkan Bulgarian, LOT, Malev, Aviogenex, Iraqi Airways and EgyptAir. The Russian Air Force also used the Tu-134 to train pilots for the Tu-22 and Tu-160 nuclear bombers.

It was also the first Soviet airliner to be permitted by the ICAO to fly international routes, but from 2002 tougher noise regulations saw the Tu-134 banned from most airports in Western Europe. Aeroflot withdrew the Tu-134 from service in 2008, when it was replaced with more modern jets including the Sukhoi SSJ100, but the type remained in use with several Aeroflot subsidiaries within Russia. The final passenger flight of the Tu-134 in Russia was on 22 May 2019 by the Siberian airline Alrosa.

Tupolev Tu-154

Country of origin: Soviet Russia.
Type: narrow-body jet airliner.
Variants: Tu-154/154A/154B/154M/154S.
First flown: 4 October 1968.
Number built: 1,026, ceased 2013.
Recent service: Aeroflot, LOT, Malev, TAROM, Cubana de Aviación.
Powerplant: 3 × 20,000lbf Kuznetsov NK-8-2U turbofans.
Span: 123ft 2in (37.55m).
Length: 157ft 6in (48.0m).
Height: 37ft 5in (11.4m).
Max cruise: 530mph (M0.69, 850kmh).
Passengers: crew 5, 114–180 passengers.
Losses: hull losses – 73, fatalities – 3,078.

Notes: A counterpart of the Boeing 727-200 and Hawker Siddeley Trident Three, the trijet Tu-154 differed from its Western lookalikes in that its Kuznetsov turbofans delivered a higher power-to-weight ratio, giving it a better take-off performance.

▼ A brace of Tupolev Tu-154M jets at Salzburg Airport on 12 January 2014. In the foreground is Aeroflot's Tu-154M, RA-85637, while in the background is Rossiya Airlines' (a subsidiary of Aeroflot) RA-85629. In passenger terms the Tu-154 was often described as an uncomfortable aircraft with a very high level of cabin noise. Each main wing gear had six-wheel bogies with large low-pressure tyres (compared to two on its rival, the Boeing 727) to facilitate operation from poorly surfaced runways. (Mike Fuchslocher/Shutterstock)

▲ Vladivostok Air Tu-154B-2, RA-85562, on the tarmac at Vladivostok Airport, 24 November 2002. Built in 1982, the aircraft was operated by Aeroflot until it was acquired in 2001 by Vladivostok Air. (Mark H. Milstein Northfoto/Shutterstock)

Its undercarriage was also far more heavy-duty to enable the Tu-154 to cope with operating from gravel or packed earth runways at some of Russia's more remote and rudimentary regional airports.

The initial prototype flew on 4 October 1968 with the first delivery of a production aircraft made to Aeroflot in early 1971, although a full commercial service did not commence until 9 February 1972 between Moscow and Mineralnye Vody. The first international services were flown on 1 August linking Moscow and Prague, with the Tu-154 destined for use on medium-length domestic and international routes.

Passenger accommodation for up to 164 was in a six-abreast configuration in two single-class cabins, separated by the galley. Other seating permutations were available. An improved version, the Tu-154A, powered by a pair of 25,350lbf Kuznetsov D-30KU engines, had extended range and payload, while the Tu-154M increased range further still to 3,600nm (6,600km).

The Tu-154 was delivered to several Soviet Bloc airlines during 1973–74, including Balkan Bulgarian and Malev, as well as Soviet-influenced Egyptair. By the end of 1974, more than 100 Tu-154s had been delivered to Aeroflot. Thirty-six years later Aeroflot announced the retirement of its Tu-154 fleet, with the final scheduled flight operating from Yekaterinburg to Moscow on New Year's Eve 2009.

Belavia, the national airline of Belarus, became the final European carrier to operate the Tu-154 in scheduled service, retiring its last two aircraft in September 2016. Russia grounded its remaining Tu-154Ms in late 2016 after a military aircraft crashed soon after take-off from Sochi on the Black Sea. All 92 people on board were killed, including 64 members of the Alexandrov Ensemble, the Russian military choir.

Yakovlev Yak-40/Yak-42

Country of origin: Soviet Russia.
Type: narrow-body jet airliners.
Variants: Yak-40/40D/40EC/40K; Yak-42/42A/42D/42ML.
First flown: Yak-40 – 21 October 1966, Yak-42 – 7 March 1975.
Number built: Yak-40 – 1,011 (ceased 1981), Yak-42 – 185 (ceased 2003).
Recent service: Aeroflot, Aviogenex, Grozny Avia, JSC Izhavia, KrasAvia, Motor Sich Airlines, Tsentr-Yug, UTair Cargo, Vologda Aviation Enterprise.
Powerplant: Yak-40 – 3 × 3,300lbf Ivchenko AI-25 turbofans, Yak-42 – 3 × 14,330lbf Lotarev D-36 turbofans.
Span: Yak-40 – 82ft 0in (25.0m), Yak-42 – 114ft 5in (34.88m).
Length: Yak-40 – 66ft 10in (20.36m), Yak-42 – 119ft 4in (36.38m).
Height: Yak-40 – 21ft 4in (6.50m), Yak-42 – 32ft 3in (9.83m).

Fuselage width: 11ft 8in (3.60m).
Max cruise: Yak-40 – 340mph (M0.45, 550kmh) at 23,000ft (7,000m), Yak-42 – 460mph (M0.60, 740kmh).
Range: Yak-40 – 970nm (1,800km), Yak-42 – 1,185nm (2,200km).
Service ceiling: Yak-40 – 26,000ft (8,000m), Yak-42 – 31,500ft (9,600m).
Passengers: Yak-40 – flight crew of 3, up to 32 passengers, Yak-42 – flight crew of 2 plus optional engineer, up to 120 passengers.
Losses: Yak-40 – hull losses – 115, fatalities – 868, Yak-42 – hull losses – 9, fatalities – 570.

▼ **Seen against a typically Russian backdrop, UTair's long-range Yakovlev Yak-42D, RA-42401, lands at Ufa International Airport in the Republic of Bashkortostan, on 27 August 2019. UTair operates scheduled domestic and some international passenger services.** (Dentorson/Shutterstock)

Notes: When the first prototype flew on 21 October 1966 the Yak-40 was the Yakovlev design bureau's maiden venture into the civil transport market, having previously been known for its fighter and trainer aircraft. The straight-wing Yak-40 was conceived as a 27-passenger short-haul feeder-liner, featuring three-abreast seating in a 2-1 configuration with an offset aisle. An emphasis on good field performance led the designers to choose a three-engine layout. The Ivchenko turbofans were specially developed for the Yak-40 and their high thrust-to-weight ratio meant they were especially suited to operating local services from high-altitude rudimentary airfields of which there are many in Russia.

Deliveries to the Soviet state airline Aeroflot began in 1968 with regular scheduled services commencing on 30 September. To meet domestic demand, production was stepped up to eight aircraft a month in 1973. Among the initial users of the Yak-42 were Aertirrena (Italy), General-Air (Hamburg), Bakhtar Afghan, Air Calypso, Balkan Bulgarian, CSA, Slov-Air and Egyptair.

With the Yak-40 as the basic production version, further developments of the design resulted in three main variants – the long-range Yak-40D; Yak-40EC – an export version that had undergone full certification to Western standards in Italy and West Germany; and the Yak-40K – a cargo/combi version with a large freight door, produced from 1975 to 1981.

Most of the 20 or so Yak-40 aircraft in service in 2020 have been repurposed for VIP/charter services, while fewer than ten remain in scheduled passenger service.

▲ Vologda Air Enterprise's Yak-40, RA-87908, climbs away from Vnukovo International Airport on 10 June 2016. (Media Works/Shutterstock)

Intended as a replacement for the Tupolev Tu-134, the first prototype of the trijet Yak-42 flew on 7 March 1975. It was almost six years before Aeroflot made the first scheduled Yak-42 passenger flight on 22 December 1980, with services following to domestic destinations from Moscow. International routes were also flown using the type from Leningrad to Helsinki and from Donetsk to Prague.

The original production version carried 120 passengers in a six-abreast 3-3 arrangement and was powered by the Soloviev D-36 turbofan. Improvements to the design resulted in three main variants – the Yak-42ML utilising modified avionics for use on international routes; Yak-40D – a long-range version that became the main production variant; and the Yak-42A developed from the Yak-42D, featuring Western avionics, spoilers and enlarged cabin door to accommodate an air bridge (also designated the Yak-142). One of the main ways in which the Yak-42 differed from the Yak-40 was with its swept wings that gave it a higher cruising speed.

In 2011, 16 airlines in Russia were operating 57 Yak-42s. By mid-2019 this number had reduced to some 22 aircraft that were being flown by regional carriers JSC Izhavia and KrasAvia.

The Yak-42 gained notoriety in 2011 when an aircraft of Yak-Service crashed on take-off into the River Volga, carrying the Lokomotiv Yaroslavl premier ice hockey team. There was only one survivor, the aircraft's flight engineer.

ILYUSHIN IL-18

Air Koryo Ilyushin Il-18D, P-835, has been used for regular domestic charter flights in North Korea. The turboprop Il-18 was a mainstay of Soviet Bloc and other client state airlines during the 1960s and '70s. Built in 1968 with the manufacturer's serial number 188011205, this aircraft was originally operated by CAAC (Air China's predecessor). Later acquired by Air Koryo, P-835 is believed to be the last remaining Il-18 in passenger service in the world. The aircraft is pictured on 1 September 2018 at Samjiyong, gateway to the North Korean sacred Mount Paektu, feted as the birthplace of leader Kim Jong-un's father, Kim Jong-il. (Saeschie Wagner/Shutterstock)

Acknowledgements

I am indebted to a great many photographers whose images grace the pages of this book. First and foremost I'd like to thank my good friend Ian Black for his help and encouragement, and for permission to use some of the superb photographs he has taken during the course of his 'day job' as an airline pilot and senior captain. Also, another friend of many years' standing, Peter R. March, for kind permission to reproduce photographs from his collection. My thanks are also due to Graham Wasey for permission to use his photograph of BA 747s at Air Salvage International, Kemble; and David Bell from Dublin for the use of his photographs taken at London-Heathrow in 1989.

The picture agency Shutterstock has been a rich source of imagery for this book and I would like to acknowledge and thank the following photographers whose work is included here – some have real names, others user names: motive56, Phuong D. Nguyen, Petr Bonek, Markus Mainka, Karlis Dambrans, Nicolas Economu, Evren Kalinbacak, Sudpoth Sirirattanasakul, Lukas Wunderlich, Nieuwland Photography, Alex Gensher, Jaroslaw Kilian, axell rf, LIAL, Jeerapan Jankaew, Corvin YO, Thiago B. Trevisan, Carlos Yudica, vaaalaa, Pawarin Prapukdee, Arjan Veltman, Eliyahu Yosef Parypa, Leony Eka Prakasa, Sundry Photography, Vytautas Kielaitis, Kenken spotter, B. Forenius, Fasttailwind, Ryan Fletcher, Ceri Breeze, Oleksandr Naumenko, NYC Russ, JL Images, faustasyan, Art Konovalov, Evgeniyqw, Media works, Denis Kabelev, Matheus Obst, Karolis Kavolelis, ER Images, QualityHD, Vladimir Zhupanenko, Heather Dunbar, Patrick Poendl, Jeffry Surianto, Renatas Repcinskas, Dennis Kartenkaemper, Mislik, nitinut80, William Howard, InsectWorld, Dentorson, Mike Fuchslocher, Mark H. Milstein Northfoto.

Thanks also to Creative Commons/Wikimedia Commons – Roland Arhelger, Bill Larkins, Micha, Airwim, Bahnfrend, Acefitt, Laurent Errera L'Union, Tim Felce, Eduard Marmet/Airliners.net, Adrian Pingstone, Aero Icarus, Aeroprints.com, Chris Lofting, Ralf Manteufel.

Sources

Magazine publications
Aerospace Technology, Airliner World, Airports of the World, Airways, Aviation Business News, Bloomberg Quint, Flight Global, Modern Airliners...

Aircraft manufacturer websites
www.airbus.com	Airbus
www.boeing.com	The Boeing Company
www.bombardier.com	Bombardier
www.embraer.com	Embraer
www.scac.ru	Sukhoi Civil Aircraft

Aviation Safety Network
www.aviation-safety.net

Enthusiast websites
www.planespotters.net
www.airliners.net
www.airfleets.net
www.b737.org.uk
www.rusaviainsider.com